KUBLAI KHAN

Lord of Xanadu

WALKER CHAPMAN

KUBLAI KHAN
Lord of Xanadu

THE BOBBS-MERRILL COMPANY, INC.

A Subsidiary of Howard W. Sams & Co., Inc.

Publishers · Indianapolis · Kansas City · New York

92-Biog
Kut

Contents

IN Xanadu did Kubla Khan
A stately pleasure-dome decree:
Where Alph, the sacred river, ran
Through caverns measureless to man
    Down to a sunless sea.
So twice five miles of fertile ground
With walls and towers were girdled round:
And there were gardens bright with sinuous rills,
Where blossomed many an incense-bearing tree;
And here were forests ancient as the hills,
Enfolding sunny spots of greenery.

           COLERIDGE: *Kubla Khan*

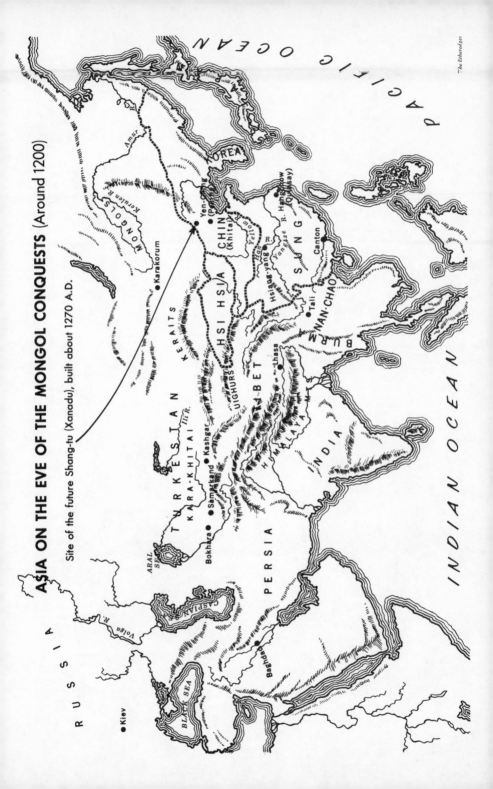

ASIA ON THE EVE OF THE MONGOL CONQUESTS (Around 1200)

Site of the future Shang-tu (Xanadu), built about 1270 A.D.

PACIFIC OCEAN

INDIAN OCEAN

RUSSIA

Kiev

BLACK SEA

CASPIAN SEA

ARAL SEA

Volga R.

Baghdad

PERSIA

TURKESTAN

KARA-KHITAI

Bokhara

Samarkand

Kashgar

Ili R.

UIGHURS

KERAITS

MONGOLS

Karakorum

Kerulen R.

Amur R.

KOREA

Yen-king (Peking)

HSI HSIA

CHIN (Khitai)

TIBET

Lhasa

HIMALAYA Mts.

INDIA

Hsiang-yang

Yel mou R.

Yellow R.

Yangtze R.

Hang-chow (Quinsay)

Canton

SUNG

Tali

NAN-CHAO

BURMA

_he Etheredges

ONE · *Marco Millions Arrives*

IN SPRING of the year 1275 a party of tired travelers from the West passed through the Great Wall of China and rejoiced, for their journey was nearly at its end. For three and a half weary years they had traveled through desert wastes and across lofty mountain passes raked by bone-chilling winds. They had outwitted brigands and triumphed over illness. And now at last they were within reach of their goal: the court of Kublai Khan, the most powerful monarch Asia had ever known.

There were three European travelers in the group, two of them shrewd and experienced, the third young, wide-eyed, exuberant. All three were men of Venice. The elder two were the brothers Niccolo and Maffeo Polo, dealers in jewels and other precious goods. This was their second trip to the domain of Kublai Khan, so the journey was a familiar one to them. But this time they had brought with them Niccolo's son Marco, who had been only seventeen when the Polos left Venice in 1271. Marco had never been away from home before. Suddenly he found himself a traveler, venturing into parts of the world nearly unknown to Europeans.

It was a rare opportunity, and Marco Polo made the most of it. Though he probably did not suspect it, more than twenty years would pass before he saw Venice again. He was destined to spend all his young manhood in the Asia ruled by Kublai Khan. He would go nearly everywhere, see almost everything—and when he returned to the city of his birth, he would write his adventures down in a book that would remain famous through the centuries.

Many things would awe Marco Polo during his long sojourn in the Orient. He came from a city that regarded itself as the most splendid in Europe; but in the fabled land of Cathay Marco would find cities so glittering that his Venice seemed shabby by comparison. He would see strange animals—crocodiles and giraffes and rhinoceroses (which he called unicorns)—and he would be shown unusual substances like asbestos and coal. He would view the workings of Kublai Khan's government from within, as a member of the monarch's own official staff. He would see the great palaces of Kublai, the spectacular hunting expeditions, all the pomp and glamor of the Khan's court.

He would travel widely, from the snow-capped mountains of Tibet to the jungles of Burma.

And when he came home to Venice, Marco Polo would tell the story of Kublai Khan's magnificence to all who cared to listen. One word above all others would stud Marco's descriptions: *milioni*, "millions." The Khan, he would say, has *milioni* of soldiers, *milioni* of subjects, *milioni* of pearls and rubies and emeralds. In Kublai's parks are *milioni* of wild animals, tigers and leopards and stags and bears. *Milioni, milioni, milioni*—the word would fall from Marco Polo's lips so often, in telling of Kublai Khan, that the people of Venice would be amused, and nickname him "Marco Millions." They would scarcely believe Marco Millions' tales of wonder.

Yet they were all true, and more besides. On his death-bed, almost fifty years after he had first arrived at the court of Kublai Khan, Marco Polo's friends asked him if the wonderful stories of his book were really true. His eyes flashed with anger and he replied heatedly, "I did not tell *one half* of what I really saw!"

When he set out from Venice with his father and uncle at the age of seventeen, Marco had no inkling of the career that lay ahead for him. He was simply embarking on the greatest adventure a young man could have. When he came home from Cathay with his head packed full of miracles, he was altogether a different person from his younger self, and yet something of that eager boy survived in the middle-aged Marco Polo who returned from Cathay. His enthusiasm never waned.

Of all the splendors of Asia, the one that impressed Marco the most was Kublai Khan himself. The moon-faced, tuft-bearded emperor was sixty years old when Marco arrived, and he had two decades of life and power still ahead of him. Wily, alert, intelligent, unendingly curious about the vast realm that was his, Kublai Khan was an unusual man and an unusual ruler. The grandson of a fierce nomad chieftain, he loved the arts and the sciences, and surrounded himself with poets, painters, and astronomers. His forebears had been content with tents of felt, but Kublai dwelled in dazzling palaces. From his grandfather and his uncle and his brother Kublai had inherited a huge empire, but he doubled its size by adding to it the sprawling land of China, which no foreigner had ever conquered before. Through the pages of Marco Polo's book runs a feeling of reverence for this complex, fascinating man. Marco tells us that Kublai is more powerful than all of his ancestors together, and then goes on to declare:

"Nay, I will say yet more; for if you were to put together all the Christians in the world, with their Emperors and their Kings, the whole of these Christians—aye, and throw in the Saracens to boot—would not have such power, or be able to do so much, as this Kublai."

The sharp eyes of Marco Polo rarely left the figure of Kublai Khan, and Kublai dominates Marco's book as he dominated Asia in his day. The best account of Kublai's life and reign is the one written by young Marco. It is not a complete picture of this many-sided ruler, for Marco loved Kublai Khan too dearly to be able to criticize him, and Kublai was not without his faults. But it is a brilliant picture, and anyone who has read the book of Marco Polo must certainly want to know more about Kublai Khan.

What were men of Venice, though, doing in the employ of the ruler of Cathay?

For an answer we must look to the tale of the elder Polos, those merchants of Venice who had blazed the trail to the Orient when Marco was still a baby. Nearly all of Asia, in the middle of the thirteenth century, was under the rule of one family: the descendants of the Mongol warrior Genghis Khan. Genghis had led his wild horsemen out of bleak Mongolia at the beginning of the century, and like a whirlwind the Mongols swept across the plains and the valleys, devouring every kingdom and state in their path, even hammering at the gates of Europe at one point. By 1260, the grandsons of Genghis Khan had come to power. One of them, Kublai, ruled much of Central Asia and China. Another, Bereke, was the commander of the Golden Horde that had conquered Russia.

Niccolo and Maffeo Polo were wealthy Venetian merchants who went back and forth from their city to Constantinople in their own ship, growing ever richer on the flow of trade between Europe and the Orient. The Polos owned a house in the Italian trading outpost of Soldaia, on the Black Sea, and in 1260 they set out on horseback from there, heading northward to the territory of Bereke Khan. They carried a store of precious jewels to sell to the Mongol overlords of Russia.

Marco Polo was taking his first toddling steps while his father and uncle were doing business at Bereke's court. If he knew his father at all, it was only as a shadowy bearded figure who had gone off on a voyage many years ago and had not yet returned. Marco went down to the docks and stared out at the dark sea, and each time a merchant vessel sailed in from Constantinople he hoped for news of the wanderers, but little news came.

While Niccolo and Maffeo were at Bereke's court, war broke out between Bereke and his cousin Hulagu, the ruler of Persia. The homeward route of the Polos was now a scene of battle. Cut off from Europe, the brothers made the best of their situation and continued eastward into the plains of Central Asia, hoping to find their way home by some new land route. For three years they sojourned in the city of Bokhara, ruled by still another grandson of Genghis Khan. They could go neither forward nor back from Bokhara, though, because all routes were made uncertain by the warfare that had burst out among the members of the Mongol royal family.

At last there came to Bokhara an embassy on its way back from Hulagu Khan in Persia, bound for the capital of the mighty Kublai, who ruled in Cathay far to the east. The Mongol ambassador spoke with the Polos, and wisely realized that Kublai would be interested in meeting a couple of clever European merchants. He invited them to join his caravan as it made its way eastward.

Even in time of war a Mongol ambassador's person was sacred, so the Polos knew they had nothing to fear if they traveled with the official party. It was a chance to get out of Bokhara, where they had been marooned so long. More than that: it was an opportunity to visit a part of the world where no man of the West had ever been before.

And so they were taken to Kublai Khan. He was "greatly pleased at their arrival," according to Marco's account, and "they were entertained with feasts and honored with other marks of distinction." Kublai questioned them in detail about European life and customs. "Above all he questioned them particularly respecting the Pope, the affairs of the Church, and the religious worship and doctrine of the Christians," Marco declares. The Polo brothers, who had learned the Mongol language, answered Kublai so well that the Khan began to consider the idea of becoming a Christian.

He asked the Polos to go back to their own land and bring him "some hundred wise men learned in the law of Christ" to instruct the Mongols. Too, he requested some holy oil from the sacred sepulcher in Jerusalem. Bearing Kublai's letter to the Pope, Niccolo and Maffeo set out for home. A golden tablet inscribed with Kublai's command was their guarantee of safe conduct wherever they went in Mongol-held territory.

The trip home lasted three years, for they were often delayed by "the extreme cold, the snow, the ice, and the flooding of the rivers." In April 1269 the Polos reached the port of Acre on the Syrian coast and learned that the Pope had just died. It might be many months before a new one was elected. They continued on to Venice to wait for the election. Coming home after an absence of more than a dozen years, Niccolo found that his wife was dead and his baby son Marco had grown into a strapping youth of fifteen. Marco's eyes glowed as his father and uncle told him wondrous stories of the Mongols and their khans.

Two years went by, and no Pope was elected to whom the Polos could deliver their message from Kublai. They decided to return to Asia without waiting further. And they took with them Niccolo's boy Marco, to his delight and our great fortune, for the elder Polos were merchants and not men of books. They never wrote a word about their travels. Marco, though, was a different sort—less of a tradesman, more of a student. He planned to take notes on everything he saw and someday to write a book about it. Unlike many travelers who make such resolutions, Marco kept his word, though he needed the help of a professional writer to get his book in order. Through Marco we know not only about the doings of the brothers Polo but about the entire world of the Mongol Empire.

By 1271 the three Polos were back in Acre. They made a pilgrimage to Jerusalem to get the holy oil. Then they learned that a Pope had finally been elected—conveniently, he was Theobald of Piacenza, the Church's representative in Acre. Theobald, now Pope Gregory X, already knew of the Polos' dealings with Kublai Khan. He could not spare the hundred priests Kublai wanted, but he offered two Dominican friars to go with the Polos and teach Christianity to the Mongols. In November 1271 the party left Acre, bound for the depths of Cathay.

Rumor of war along the route frightened the two friars, and it was not long before they decided to turn back. Marco, Niccolo, and Maffeo plunged on undaunted. Ever eastward they journeyed, past Armenia's Mount Ararat, where Noah's Ark had come to rest; past the storied cities of Mosul and Baghdad; into Persia, through fertile plains and salt-fouled deserts; and on to the city of Badakshan, where fresh winds whipped mountain air into their lungs. The hot deserts of Persia had sapped Marco's strength, and he was ill by the time he came to Badakshan. The Polos remained there a full year while he recovered.

Then it was onward, to the icy mountains of the Pamirs. There Marco discovered the wild sheep with immense horns which are known to this day as *Ovis Poli*, "the sheep of Polo." Always the keen observer, Marco noted in the frosty Pamirs that "on account of this great cold, fire does not burn so clearly, nor is it of the same color as elsewhere, and it cooks food less well." The altitude, not the temperature, was the real cause of the fire's weakness, but at least Marco had his eyes open.

Now the Polos were traveling the Old Silk Road, where for thirteen centuries caravans had passed between China and the West. They saw the cities of Kashgar, Yarkand, and Khotan, rich with jade and gems, and left them behind to enter the grim desert of the Gobi, said to be haunted by phantoms and nameless terrors. To the right and the left of the caravan track lurked unknown spirits, and strange sounds were heard afar—the tinkling of invisible bells, the beat of mysterious drums. The Polos plodded forward, unscathed by demons. The borders of Kublai's realm drew near. To the travelers' left was barren Mongolia; to the right lay populous China. They followed the frontier line, probably traveling just within the Great Wall of China, although strangely enough Marco never mentions in his book that monumental ribbon of stone.

By this time Kublai Khan had heard of the approach of the Venetians, for no one entered his country unnoticed. Messengers riding night and day had brought word to him that his friends the Polo brothers were returning after nine years, and that they had brought with them a young man of their family. Kublai sent a welcoming party, which encountered the Polos when they were still forty days' journey from the capital. And, Marco reports, the three travelers "were honorably entertained upon the road, and supplied with all that they required."

In May 1275, Marco Polo arrived at the city of Shang-tu, summer capital of Kublai Khan.

Shang-tu (which the English poet Samuel Taylor Coleridge called *Xanadu*) left young Marco staggered by its opulence. "In this city," he wrote many years later, "Kublai Khan had an immense palace made of marble and stone, with halls and rooms all gilt and adorned with figures of beasts and birds, and pictures of trees and flowers of different kinds. It is most wondrously beautiful and marvelously decorated. On one side it is bounded by the city-wall, and from that point another wall runs out enclosing a space of no less than sixteen miles, with numerous springs and rivers and meadows. And the Great Khan keeps all kinds of animals in it, namely stags and fallow-deer and roe-bucks."

Presiding over all this splendor was the Khan himself, plump, stately, vigorous despite his sixty years. Kublai felt well pleased with himself at the moment. He was on the verge of completing the conquest of China, a task that had occupied him for a quarter of a century. The end of the war was in sight. Most of China was already under Mongol control, and the child who had inherited the Dragon Throne of China was powerless. Soon, Kublai knew, he would be not only the Great Khan of the Mongols but Emperor of China as well, fulfilling a lifelong dream.

So he greeted the Polos in a jovial frame of mind. They appeared at the imperial palace and found the Great Khan surrounded by his nobles. Niccolo and Maffeo fell on their knees before him. Marco, almost stupefied with wonder, did the same. Kublai gestured to the three Venetians to rise. He asked Niccolo and Maffeo how they had fared since they had left his court in 1266. The Polo brothers said they had fared well, and were pleased to find the Khan flourishing and healthy. They presented Kublai the letters of the Pope, at which he showed great delight. Next they produced the holy oil from Jerusalem, for which Kublai thanked them graciously. At last the Great Khan noticed the young Marco standing silently to one side.

"Who is that in your company?" he inquired.

Niccolo replied, "Sire, he is my son and your servant."

"He is welcome," declared Kublai, "and much it pleases me."

Telling his own tale, Marco writes, "And why should I make a long story? There was much rejoicing at the court because of [our] arrival, and [we] met with attention and honor from everybody."

Kublai was glad to see his old friends Niccolo and Maffeo once again, but it was Marco who particularly interested him. Kublai and Marco were different as different could be, the one a sixty-year-old Oriental potentate, the other a youth of scarcely more than twenty from a city of Europe. But they shared one common trait: a feverish curiosity, a boundless desire to know all about the world. Kublai was quick to recognize this trait in Marco. He smiled to see the young man asking many questions, studying languages, taking notes of Mongol customs. He called Marco to his side and they spoke for long hours, the Khan questioning Marco about Europe, and Marco just as earnestly daring to question the Khan about Mongol life.

As lord of half the world, Kublai was in a fine position to feed his curiosity with facts about strange and remote places. Yet, as he told Marco, he had had difficulties in getting the information he wanted. He sent ambassadors to all parts of Asia, but when they returned they spoke only of the official business they had transacted and told him nothing about the customs and unusual features of the lands they had visited. Such ambassadors, Kublai told Marco, were nothing but fools and dunces. "I would rather hear about the strange things and the manners of the different countries you have seen than merely be told of the business you went upon," Kublai angrily said to these envoys.

Marco agreed. What was the use of traveling to a distant place, he wondered, if you did not bring back information about its way of life and the unusual creatures and plants found there? He himself would not be so foolish as to blind his eyes to such matters. It occurred to Kublai, therefore, that Marco might be a useful ambassador, since he spoke several languages, was wise beyond his years, and had the wonderful gift of curiosity.

Thus began Marco Polo's career as a representative of Kublai Khan. Kublai sent him as an envoy to a country six months' journey away, and Marco returned with a full account of all the unusual things he had seen. The Emperor was charmed, and remarked to his courtiers, "If this young man lives, he cannot fail to prove himself a man of sound judgment and true worth."

For seventeen years Marco served the Khan. Then he and his father and uncle returned to Venice, homesick at last, arriving in 1295 after a three-year journey. On that homeward voyage the sad news reached them of Kublai Khan's death. The Polos went to Venice and told their tales, and Marco won his nickname "Marco Millions." In 1298 he went to sea during a naval war between the rival cities of Venice and Genoa and was captured; in prison he had the leisure to write the book he had promised to give the world. An author of chivalrous romances, Rustichello, was in the same prison, and Marco dictated his book to him. Rustichello gave it courtly phrases, but the material itself is Marco's.

The hero of that book is the Great Khan Kublai. No man ever served Kublai Khan more loyally, or was devoted more wholeheartedly to him, than Marco Millions of Venice. Marco knew the Khan during the greatest years of his power. He saw the Mongols at their summit; the decline of their dynasty came swiftly once Kublai vanished from the scene. The century of Mongol rule caused all the world to shake, for at one point it seemed that the entire globe might come under the rule of the family of Genghis

Khan. It did not happen, and Kublai Khan was partly responsible for the failure of the Mongols to conquer the world because he had other ideas. But for a time the men of Europe shivered in their boots for fear of the Mongol hordes, and the course of history was forever changed in many ways by what happened in Mongolia at the start of the thirteenth century.

Kublai Khan, then, was something more than a picturesque ruler of a faraway land. He was the most glorious member of a dynamic family. The wonderful book of Marco Polo introduces us to Kublai Khan—but if we are to know more about him, and to understand the line from which he sprang, we must turn back in time to the dawn of Mongol greatness, to the founder of the dynasty, the ferocious Genghis Khan.

TWO · *Genghis the Mighty*

ABOUT 1167, a boy named Temujin was born to a tribal chieftain's wife on the banks of the Amur River in Eastern Asia. His father, Yesukai, led one of the many small bands of nomads known as Mongols who roamed the dismal wastelands north of China. Little Temujin came into the world clutching a lump of clotted blood in his tiny fist, and the medicine man of the tribe said it was an omen that he would become a mighty warrior.

The omen was read correctly. Under the name Genghis Khan, Temujin would lead the Mongols to greatness and establish the world's most far-flung empire. From the Pacific to the Mediterranean, all men would bow to Mongol commands one day. But who could foresee such a thing? Who could imagine that the Mongols would ever know such grandeur?

The promise of greatness did not seem to be there. The Persian historian Juvaini, who was born in the year Genghis Khan died and lived at the royal court in Mongol-conquered Persia, wrote that "Before the appearance of Genghis Khan the Mongols had no chief or ruler. Each tribe or two tribes lived separately; they were not united with one another, and there was constant fighting and hostility between them. Some of them regarded robbery and violence, immorality and debauchery, as deeds of manliness and excellence. The Khan of Khitai [Northern China] used to demand and seize goods from them. Their clothing was of the skins of dogs and mice, and their food was the flesh of those animals and other dead things."

The Mongols were wanderers, raising herds of horses for their livelihood and drifting from pasture to pasture, pitching their felt tents wherever the grazing was good. Family groups clung together, and perhaps a thousand of these small clans existed, with little friendship among them.

Though they were similar in language and customs, the many Mongol tribes showed no desire for political unity. Spread out over a vast region of Asia, they had little contact with one another. Now and again some strong chieftain succeeded in bringing several Mongol tribes into a confederation. Yesukai, the father of Temujin, had built such a confederation out of the group of Mongol tribes called the Tatars or Tartars. But these unions never survived beyond the lifetime of the strong leaders who created them.

By race the Mongols were related to the Chinese, the Japanese, and other Oriental peoples, but their centuries of harsh nomadic life had hardened them, making them stocky and tough, with big bodies and short limbs. John of Plano Carpini, an Italian friar who visited the Mongol homeland in 1246, wrote that "The Mongols or Tartars, in outward shape, are unlike to all other people. For they are broader between the eyes, and the balls of their cheeks, than men of other nations be. They have flat and small noses, little eyes, and eyelids standing straight upright. They are shaven on the crowns of their heads like priests. They wear their hair somewhat longer about their ears than upon their forehead, but behind they let it grow long like woman's hair."

These Mongols were simple people who knew nothing of reading or writing, took baths no more often than rivers ran upstream, and lived on the milk and meat their herds supplied. They greased their bodies to keep off the cold and rode like fiends, their stubby legs clinging to the bellies of their steeds for hour after hour. During the long, bitter winters they stayed close to their *yurts* or tents, which Marco Polo relates "are circular, and are made of wands covered with felts. These are carried along with them whithersoever they go; for the wands are so strongly bound together, and likewise so well combined, that the frame can be made very light." Milk and animal grease were used to thicken the felt coverings as a shield against the cold; a fire burned within, with an opening in the roof to let out the smoke, but we can be sure that the interior of a Mongol *yurt* was a dark, smoky, rancid-smelling place. The Mongols had no objection to the odors about them, though their sense of smell, like all their other senses, was unusually keen. These men of the barren plains were sharp of eye, swift to smell anything unusual. They needed keen senses. Enemies were everywhere. Raiders from another tribe might come to steal horses; no man could relax.

Riders patrolled the pastures, their eyes endlessly searching the horizon for danger. Behind their shoulders dangled lances or long, wickedly curved swords. At their left hips rested hand-axes and bows; on their right side were the quivers of arrows. A Mongol could gallop and aim his bow at the same time, to deadly effect.

When they were not defending their pastures from marauders or rounding up their herds, the Mongols relaxed with *khumiss*, an alcoholic drink made from the fermented milk of mares. Marco Polo drank it and liked it: "You would take it for white wine," he said, "and a right good drink it is." Gathering about the flickering fires in their smoky tents, the Mongols quaffed *khumiss* by the quart, until it made them drunk, and they leaped and pranced and shouted. While the young men lurched to and fro in clumsy dances, their hide boots clumping against the

ground, the elders chanted tales of great Mongols of the
past, the legendary *Borjigun* or "Blue-eyed Men" of long
ago, whose voices had rolled like thunder in the mountains, whose hands had been as strong as the paws of bears.

Young Temujin listened to these tales of ancient heroes
and dreamed of a day when the Mongols at their tipsy
festivals would sing of his own great deeds. The *khumiss*
bowl was passed again and again, and even the young ones
drank. There were few other pleasures in the world for
them. With a bowlful of mare's milk in his belly, every
man could imagine himself a world-bestriding colossus.

When Temujin was nine, his father Yesukai took him
on a long journey to the West. It was time, according to
Mongol custom, for Temujin to take a wife. Father and
son rode out into the grassy plains, through dark forests
and over high mountains, until they came to a lake where
a tribe belonging to the group of Mongol tribes known as
the Jungirats was camped. Yesukai explained their quest to
Dai Sechen—Dai the Wise—the Jungirat chieftain. He
had a daughter, Bortei, nine years old like Temujin. Dai
Sechen studied the boy, watched him on his horse, wheel-
ing and turning, letting go of the reins to shower arrows in
all directions like a full-grown warrior. It was an impressive display. Temujin was a child, but he rode like a man,
and his lean, hard body rippled with strength. His eyes
were like the eyes of a cat, seeing everything, revealing
nothing.

Temujin was betrothed to Bortei and remained in the

land of the Jungirats to seal the alliance between Yesukai's tribe and the tribe of Dai Sechen. He lived there three years, and learned for the first time of the country called Khitai (which Marco knew as Cathay) in the south. Khitai had once been part of the great realm of China. But about the year 900, a race of nomad warriors called the Khitan poured down out of the north, overthrew the Chinese rulers, and became masters of the northern part of China. The Khitan in time grew soft and fat in the luxurious cities of China. About forty years before Temujin was born, another northern tribe, the Jurchen, invaded Khitai and seized control.

The Jurchen were in power now, Temujin learned. Their rulers called themselves the Chin ("Golden") Dynasty. They lived in great cities ringed by gigantic walls and enjoyed vast wealth, enormous treasure, high prosperity. The people of Khitai, who were Chinese, toiled without rest to keep their Chin overlords comfortable.

Temujin considered all this. The Jurchen invaders, and the Khitan before them, had been no more than horse-raising nomads. Yet they had been able to conquer half of China. Why could not the Mongols do what these other tribes had done in the past? What was the secret of the Jurchen and Khitan strength?

Organization, Temujin realized. The two conquering tribes had each been tightly bound by laws and oaths to serve a single plan of conquest. But the Mongols were scattered and weak, divided into hundreds of petty clans. How had the earlier conquerors become strong? Because, Temujin discovered, one man with vision had unified them. The Khitan had come under the rule of a warrior named A-pao-chi in 907, and he had made them great. The rise of the Jurchen was the work of the chieftain A-ku-ta, who defied the Khitan in 1112 and defeated them ten years later.

One man, one man with strength and foresight, Temujin thought——

Why not one man to unify the Mongols, as A-pao-chi had done for the Khitan and A-ku-ta for the Jurchen?

Temujin saw himself as that man. Suppose his father could complete the task of bringing together the Tartar tribes, and Dai Sechen, his father-in-law, could unite the Jungirats. Then Temujin, the heir to both groups, would have the nucleus of a powerful striking force. He had only to close his eyes and he could see himself at the head of an army of thousands of horsemen, thundering across the plains to loot the wealthy cities of Khitai.

It was a bold dream for any man, and an absurd dream for a boy not yet thirteen. But there came a cruel awakening. A Tartar messenger rode into the Jungirat camp bearing dark news: Yesukai had been poisoned by enemies, and Temujin must return to his home tribe at once.

He left Bortei with her father, because their marriage had not yet been officially celebrated, and hurried home to find Yesukai dead and his tent echoing with the sobs of the mourners. It seemed the end of Temujin's vivid dream. His father had brought many related tribes under one rule, but in the instant of his death all those tribes gathered their herds and broke away in different directions. Temujin, only a boy, was powerless to make them obey him. The confederation his father had forged over many years was shattered in a day.

Of all Yesukai's horde of followers, only his immediate family remained. The dead man had had two wives, according to Mongol custom, and they had borne him six sons and several daughters. Temujin was the eldest son of the first wife, and so was considered Yesukai's heir and successor. His full brother Kasar supported him. But his half-brothers Bektor and Belgutai were troublemakers. Bektor and Belgutai together were stronger than Temujin and Kasar. When the four young Mongols went hunting for food, Bektor and Belgutai often seized more than their share.

Temujin was furious. If he could not maintain authority in his own family, how could he dare to dream of being lord of magnificent Khitai? He resolved to do a terrible deed. One day when Belgutai went out fishing alone, Temujin called to Kasar. They pursued the other half-brother, Bektor, and Temujin killed him with a single arrow.

His mother boiled with rage. "You are like wolves," she told her two sons, "like mad dogs that tear their own flesh. What have you done? Our only friends are our own shadows. We have no weapons but our own hands, and you have lopped off two of these hands and annihilated one of these shadows." But the unruly Bektor was dead, and Belgutai lost no time making peace with Temujin.

Hard years followed. New Mongol leaders had arisen to replace Yesukai, and Temujin and his family, who represented a threat to the power of these new chieftains, became fugitives. They lived in the woods, ate rats and fish, guarded their few horses against their enemies. Several times Temujin came close to losing his life. But he won a few followers during this time of forest life—other fugitives, who were impressed with Temujin's valor and strength and who were awed by the young man's iron determination to regain the power that had been his father's. By the time he was seventeen, Temujin headed a hard-riding band of fearless young Mongols. When the *khumiss* bowls began to pass, men now sang of Temujin's deeds, and his name was known from one end of Mongolia to the other.

Temujin had not forgotten his bride. After an absence of four years, Temujin rode to the Jungirat camp, accompanied by his half-brother Belgutai. Dai Sechen greeted them warmly. Bortei came forth, now a young woman who had many times wondered if she would ever see her betrothed again. She found Temujin tall and powerful, stern of expression, a man who spoke few words but said nothing unwise. The wedding was a joyous feast that lasted for days.

Temujin had come into his time of greatness. Men from

many tribes joined his horde. He built a network of followers, linking family and family, clan and clan, tribe and
tribe, using a system of blood-brotherhood to rivet his
forces together under his command. But there still were
many who would not yield to Temujin. A tribe called the
Merkits defied him—and made so bold as to raid the Mongol camp, carrying off Temujin's own wife while he was
absent!

Bortei was gone, and Temujin did not think his forces
were strong enough to regain her. Swallowing his pride,
he made a somber journey westward to the land of the
Kerait tribe. They were nomads who had become Christians, and Temujin's father Yesukai had been blood-
brother to the Kerait leader. Now Temujin presented himself, reminded the Keraits of that old alliance, and asked
for help. The Kerait ruler, Togrul Khan, gladly adopted
Temujin as his son and put soldiers at his disposal.

Temujin attacked the Merkits and destroyed them. The
men were slain, the women were made slaves. He found
his Bortei unharmed, but not alone. During her captivity
she had given birth to a son. It was an unwelcome discov-
ery for Temujin, for he could not be sure he was the father
of the child. But he accepted the boy as his own, and
named him Juchi, "the guest."

Other sons followed as the years passed—Chagadai,
Ogodai, Tului. Thousands of warriors rode behind the
banners of Temujin. Where he could, Temujin won the

backing of other tribes through diplomacy and cunning.
When that failed him, he smashed them with direct force.
By the time he was forty years old, no tribe in Mongolia
denied his authority. Temujin had achieved his dream. He
had pieced together hundreds of scattered clans and tribes
to create a true empire in the land of nomad horsemen.

In the year 1206—the Year of the Panther by the Chinese calendar that the Mongols had borrowed for their
own use—a great *khuriltai*, or meeting of every tribe, was
held on the banks of the Kerulen River in central Mongolia. A splendid pavilion was raised, with golden plates
decorating the wooden pillars that supported the roof. The
white flag of Temujin fluttered beside the entrance. Behind
the leader's tent were the tents of his trusted comrades, his
generals and lieutenants, and beyond these the tents of
Temujin's soldiers and their families stretched as far as the
eye could see.

The khuriltai had been called to mark officially the supremacy of Temujin over all of Mongolia. Temujin appeared before his tent, and the Mongol princes knelt
before him, loudly crying out, begging him to accept their
throne. He would no longer be known as Temujin, but as
Genghis, the "universal ruler."

Among the Mongols any chieftain wore the title *khan*,
"prince." Genghis Khan, though, would have a special
rank: *Khaghan*, or Khan of Khans, Great Khan. There
might be many khans among the Mongols at any one time,

but there would be but one Khaghan, and he would be of the family of Genghis, the Great Khan.

And it was so. The khans of the Mongols swore to obey the Great Khan in all things, and Genghis accepted their homage. He spoke of his vision of conquest: "Man's highest joy is in victory," Genghis told the khuriltai. "To conquer one's enemies, to pursue them, to deprive them of their possessions, to make their beloved weep, to ride on their horses, and to embrace their wives and daughters."

Genghis Khan was declaring war against the entire world. He would not rest, he said, until men everywhere obeyed the word of the Mongols. It was not the first time in human history, or the last, that one man had set out to conquer every nation. Alexander the Great, Napoleon, Hitler, and others had the same dream, though none came so close to fulfilling it as Genghis Khan. We may wonder about his motives. Mere wealth did not tempt him, for he scorned luxuries and kept to the simple ways of his people. He was capable of cruelty, but he had no real wish to do harm to others for its own sake. He was far from being a bloodthirsty madman, nor was he a tyrant who made his subjects groan in slavery.

Why, then, conquer the world?

Perhaps it was because he did not know how to stop. The whole impulse of his life had been one of building an empire, and he had not halted after he had welded one clan to another, tribe to tribe. By the time Mongolia was his, he was riding a juggernaut that could not be slowed. Ceaseless warfare, endless outward expansion—only thus could the empire be held together at all. So Genghis looked toward this land and that, planning to add them to his domain, and after those had been taken there were the nations yet beyond, and so onward to all horizons.

Perhaps, too, his nomad nature had a love of simplicity that could only be satisfied by world conquest. Genghis Khan looked upon the world and saw it full of many nations, each with its own code of laws (usually disregarded), its own language, its own rulers. How much more orderly things would be if all were under one central authority! Out of the turmoil of a divided world Genghis could bring a neatly organized structure, harmonious and satisfying.

As a foundation for his world empire, Genghis proclaimed a code of laws, the *yasas*. The Persian chronicler Juvaini tells us: "In accordance and agreement with his own mind he established a rule for every occasion and a regulation for every circumstance; while for every crime he fixed a penalty. And since the Tartar peoples had no script of their own, he gave orders that Mongol children should learn writing from the Uighur [a Turkish tribe]; and that these *yasas* and ordinances should be written down on rolls. These rolls are called the *Great Book of Yasas* and are kept in the treasury of the chief princes."

All tribes were to be united as one. Tartars, Jungirats,

Keraits, Oirats, Urianguts, and all the rest would be known simply as Mongols, the general name for these nomad horsemen. And all would obey the *yasas*, which came down from heaven on high through the person of the divinely chosen Great Khan.

Every Mongol was to consider himself a soldier. Men between fourteen and seventy were chosen for active duty, some to fight, some to care for the roads and the horses. Women, boys, old men, and weaklings were given the tasks of maintaining the pastures and the home encampments. The Mongol army was built out of groups of ten men, drawn from different tribes in such a way as to replace the old tribal loyalties with a new loyalty to the Mongol state. One man of each ten was the leader of the group; every unit of ten was part of a unit of a hundred men, with its own leader, and units of a thousand and ten thousand warriors were formed from these. At the top of this pyramid were a hundred or so great commanders, reporting directly to Genghis Khan. The organization was tight and efficient; no man could shirk his duty, none could do less than his share. If any soldier betrayed his trust, his commander was held responsible, and even a commander of ten thousand might suffer for the faults of an underling. The highest leaders might be degraded if they allowed discipline to slacken; on the other hand, a man of the ranks might reach the upper levels swiftly if he distinguished himself in battle. No wages were paid; the individual

Mongol was simply a cog in the machine of war, and would receive food and all essentials from the general supply so long as he obeyed the *yasas*.

In spring and autumn the men hunted, for food and for sport. In the summer they fought against unruly tribes on the borders of the Mongol-held domain while the women remained in the home camps, guarded by a detachment of troops. Genghis sent one army to the west and one to the east each year, and surrounded himself with a small picked band of the finest warriors, ten thousand in all, the elite corps of the Mongols. Such an elite force was known as an *ordo*. When the Mongol *ordos* began to invade Europe years later, Europeans turned the word into *hordes* and spoke of the Mongols as if their numbers were boundless, like "grasshoppers covering the face of the earth." But actually the Mongol "hordes" that conquered so much of the world were quite small. At the height of his power, Genghis Khan never commanded more than some 250,000 men, and only half of these were Mongols, the rest allies from other nations. When the Mongols conquered China, their total population was no greater than two million, as against a hundred million Chinese.

The secret of Mongol might was their iron discipline and superb horsemanship, not the great numbers that a frightened Europe imagined to exist. "They are excellent soldiers," wrote Marco Polo, "and passing valiant in battle. They are also more capable of bearing hardships than other nations; for many a time, if need be, they will go for a month without any supply of food, living only on the milk of their mares and on such game as their bows will win them. . . . When they are going on a distant expedition they take no gear with them except two leather bottles for milk; a little earthenware pot to cook their meat in; and a little tent to shelter them from rain. And in case of great urgency they will ride ten days on end without lighting a fire or taking a meal."

Mongol boys learned to ride almost as soon as they could walk. They trained their horses so well that beast seemed part of man, both under the command of a single brain. A Mongol steed could wheel and charge with the greatest agility—"just like a dog," according to Marco—while its master fired arrows with phenomenal speed and accuracy, arrows that could slay at a distance of two hundred yards. In battle, the Mongols burst forward in well-ordered columns, showering arrows with such ferocity that their terrified victims bolted in panic; the horsemen maneuvered their foes into a herd, ringing them for the slaughter. Where the enemy refused to panic, the Mongols would pretend to retreat, drawing their opponents after them. Then, at a given signal, they would swing around and charge once more, uttering terrifying cries. "In this sort of warfare," Marco Polo commented, "the adversary imagines he has gained a victory, when in fact he has lost the battle."

The world had never before seen a military machine of such perfection. A Mongol army moved in total coordination, following a design laid down in advance and never varying from the commands its leaders issued. "They are rather monsters than men," wrote an English monk in 1240, "thirsting and drinking blood, tearing and devouring the flesh of dogs and men; clothed with ox-hides, armed with iron plates; in stature thick and short, well set, strong in body; in war invincible, in labor infatigable. . . ."

Genghis had proved himself a great builder. He inspired an almost supernatural awe in his men, and they were willing to follow him to the ends of the earth. In 1206, when he was named Great Khan, he and his Mongols controlled a realm stretching a thousand miles from east to west, six hundred miles from north to south. But that was just the beginning.

He looked westward toward Tibet, where a kingdom known in Chinese as the Hsi-Hsia had been established. By 1209 the Mongols were masters there. Two years later, Genghis marched against China, hammering at the walls of the Chin Dynasty capital of Yenching, the modern Peking. The Chin troops were no match for the Mongols, but Yenching's titanic walls could hold back even Genghis Khan. Not until 1215, when traitors within the city opened its gates to the Mongols, did Yenching fall to Genghis. The splendid capital was looted and burned, as a warning to the other walled cities of China. The Chin Emperor fled, allowing Genghis to occupy much of his domain.

Among the many prizes of conquest was an imperial adviser named Yeh-lu Ch'u-ts'ai, who was taken by Mongol soldiers when Yenching fell. He was a Khitan, a member of the royal house of conquerors that had been overthrown a hundred years before by the Chin, but despite this he had served the Chin Emperor to the best of his abilities. When he came before Genghis, the Great Khan was greatly impressed by the wisdom, courage, and honesty of Yeh-lu Ch'u-ts'ai. Genghis took him into his own service—a significant step, for the clever minister had much to offer the rugged, simple barbarian conquerors.

New adventures called Genghis westward—to wage war in Tibet and Turkestan, to the borders of Persia, to the frontiers of India. The legend of Mongol might preceded the invaders into these countries. The dread of the Mongols was so intense by now that they met with little resistance. Strong men were paralyzed by the mere thought that the Mongols were coming. "So great was the fear that Allah put into all hearts," wrote the Arab historian Ibn Athir, "that things happened that are hard to believe. Someone told me that a Mongol rode alone into a village with many people and set himself to kill them, one after another, without a person daring to defend himself. I heard also that one Mongol, wishing to kill a prisoner of his and finding himself without a weapon, ordered his captive to lie down. He went to look for a sword, with which he killed the unfortunate, who had not moved.

"Someone said to me, 'I was on the road with seventeen

other men. We saw a Mongol horseman come up to us. He ordered us to tie up our companions, each man to bind the other's arms behind his back. The others were beginning to obey him, when I said to them, "This man is alone. Let us kill him and escape." They replied, "We are too much afraid." "But this man will kill you," I said. "Let's do for him, and perhaps Allah will preserve us." But not one of the seventeen dared do it. So I killed the Mongol with a blow of my knife. We all ran away and saved ourselves.' "

In bringing Mongol justice to the rest of the world, Genghis brought terrible slaughter—but always in the name of his great plan. Monstrous though the crimes of the Mongols were, they were rarely committed for the sake of sheer brutality. Their purpose was to spread terror and make further conquests easier. But once a district was brought under control, all atrocities ceased, and the rule of Genghis' *yasas* was imposed. Mongols who indulged in butchery that served no political purpose were put to death by their own commanders.

Outward swept the Mongol tide. The rulers of the conquered lands were slain and their people became vassals of the Mongols. Genghis could not be everywhere at once, of course, and his four sons came to play important roles in the campaigns of conquest. These were the sons of Bortei, who would be his heirs; he had other sons by other wives, and they were respected among the Mongols, but they would never inherit high rank or power. Juchi was the eldest of Bortei's children, the one who had been born while his mother was a Merkit captive. Because no one was certain that Juchi was Genghis' son, he lived under a shadow of doubt, and grew restless and bitter. Genghis made him the leader of the troops that struck deep into the cold northern steppes of the far west. He kept his other sons—Chagadai, Ogodai, Tului—closer to him.

Tului, the youngest of the sons, was the fiercest in battle. Juvaini's chronicle tells what happened when Tului invaded the province of Khorasan, along the Old Silk Road: "With one stroke a world which billowed with fertility was laid desolate, and the regions thereof became a desert, and the greater part of the living dead, and their skin and bones crumbling dust; and the mighty were humbled and immersed in the calamities of perdition." Mounted on a golden throne, Tului directed the onslaught against these walled cities, using machines built by Chinese engineers that hurled stones against the walls and flung firebrands over them. Ogodai and Chagadai were fearless warriors and brilliant generals also, though they were both too fond of the *khumiss* bowl, and often were found roaring with drunkenness.

The great fear of Genghis Khan was that his empire would be divided after his death—that his sons might quarrel and split away from one another. Already he had put each at the head of an army of his own, and it was easy to see that the four sons might stake out claims in separate quarters of the empire. Before he gave them their assignments, Genghis called his sons together and showed them a quiver of arrows. He drew an arrow out, and snapped it in half. He drew out two arrows, and snapped them the same way. Then he pulled forth a thick handful of arrows, and handed them to Juchi, the eldest.

"Break them," he said.

But Juchi could not, nor could Chagadai, nor Ogodai, nor Tului, for it was beyond the strength of even the strongest man to snap so many arrows at once.

"So it is with you also," Genghis told them. "Not even mighty warriors can break a frail arrow when it is multiplied and supported by its fellows. Therefore, as long as you brothers support one another and render assistance to one another, your enemies can never gain the victory over you. But if you fall away from one another, you can be broken as I broke the arrows, one at a time."

The brothers went their separate ways—Juchi to the mountainous country of the far northwest, Chagadai to the rich Silk Road cities of the west, Ogodai to the occupied part of China. Tului, having returned from his savage campaigns in the west, now settled in Mongolia, guarding the home territories, as the youngest son was required to do by ancient Mongol tradition.

In 1225, feeling age heavy upon him, Genghis Khan called a great khuriltai to decide the question of his successor. To all the Mongol khans went the special messengers, called "arrow" messengers because they were so swift. They rode day and night, their bodies bandaged to give them protection against cold. These men slept in the saddle, changed horses whenever they came to an encampment, and traveled like the wind; they would cover in a few days distances that ordinarily took weeks. And one by one the sons of Genghis headed for the khuriltai.

All but Juchi in his distant mountainous realm. He sent word that he was ill, and could not come. Genghis was enraged; it violated the *yasas* to refuse to attend a khuriltai. Word reached him that Juchi had been seen hunting, and so could not be ill. Lying to the Great Khan! Tongues wagged in the Mongol camps; it was said that Juchi was defiant because men doubted he was a true son of Genghis Khan, and that now that he was master of his own territory he would mingle no more with other Mongols. Genghis ordered Ogodai and Chagadai to lead troops to bring Juchi under control. Civil war threatened among the Mongols. Then came later news: Juchi had indeed been sick, and now Juchi was dead. There had been no rebellion against the *yasas* after all. Genghis remained alone for two days in his tent, mourning his dead son and praying Juchi's pardon for the injustice that had been done him.

Then the khuriltai of 1225 was held. Genghis confirmed the earlier division of responsibility in the empire. Chagadai would govern Central Asia; Ogodai would have China, Tibet, and other conquered territories in that part of the world; Tului was to continue guarding the frontiers of the vast Mongol homeland. The far country, up to the frontiers of Russia, would go to Juchi's eldest son Batu, the first of the grandsons of Genghis Khan to win power.

The realm was not to be divided into separate countries, though. There would still be a Great Khan, and his word would be law wherever Mongols reigned. But which of the three sons would inherit the throne? Chagadai was the eldest surviving son, but he was a cold man, lacking in charity and mercy. Tului was the boldest warrior and the most vigorous leader, but he was also the youngest son, and it was poor policy to give the throne to the youngest, while passing over his brothers.

That left Ogodai—strong, good-natured, generous. He was not as clever as Tului, or as strong of purpose as Chagadai. His mind was frequently fogged by drink. But he was a man that other men could love and respect. He had the qualities of leadership, which meant that he could compromise and bargain as well as command. Chagadai was too harsh to rule, Tului too fiery.

Before he declared his decision, Genghis told his sons and grandsons another parable: "There once was a serpent with one tail and many heads, and another serpent with one head and many tails. When the cold of winter came, they both had to find a safe place to hide. For the many-headed serpent, every crevice was too narrow. The heads quarreled with one another, until finally each had to find a hole for itself. The body had to remain outside, exposed to the cold. It perished, and all the heads died with it. But the many-tailed serpent cuddled all its tails beneath its one head, and thus was able to survive the winter." The old warrior looked down the ranks of his many descendants. They were the tails of the Mongol serpent; but there could be only one head. "Which among you shall inherit my realm?" he asked.

And he answered, "I make Ogodai my heir, and place the keys of the empire in the hand of his valor and ability."

He explained his reasoning. The sons listened, and none of them dared object. Tului was deeply disappointed, because he regarded himself as the most capable man of the three. But he agreed to obey his father's word. So did Chagadai. Only Ogodai, the newly designated heir, seemed unwilling. He knelt humbly and said, "O my ruler and father, you have commanded me to speak. I must not say that I will not take over the succession, and I shall endeavor to rule with zeal and wisdom. But I fear that my children may lack the capacity to inherit the throne after me."

Genghis Khan made it clear that he did not intend the highest power to remain in the hands of Ogodai's own descendants forever. Whenever a Great Khan died, his successor was to be chosen by a khuriltai from among all the qualified members of Genghis Khan's descendants, the *Altyn Uruk* or "Golden Family." If no son of Ogodai were worthy, the khuriltai could turn to a different branch of Genghis' family. Always, Genghis stressed, the new ruler must be chosen by a khuriltai, and every Mongol must attend the gathering, without exception.

The division had been made. The transfer of power now could take place peacefully when Genghis Khan's life was ended. Until then, he would continue to lead his hordes on the unfinished business of the empire, for many lands remained to be subjugated.

He dismissed the khuriltai, telling his sons, "Believe no one, trust no enemy, help and support one another amid the dangers of life, obey the *yasas*, and carry to an end any action you may begin. I have spoken. Now return to your armies."

Less than two years later the Great Khan was dead. The illness that had been upon him when he called the khuriltai grew worse, and on the eighteenth of August 1227, in the Year of the Pig, Genghis Khan died while leading a campaign in the hills of the Hsi-Hsia country. In autumn his body was carried northward into Mongolia and buried in a secret place known only to a few.

The hand that had guided the Mongols in their tempestuous rise toward greatness had let slip the reins. Now it remained to be seen whether the sons of Genghis Khan could seize control—or whether the vast empire would fly apart.

THREE · *The Mongol Empire*

THE FIRST time that the boy who would become Kublai Khan saw his famous grandfather Genghis, he was nine years old. That was in the year 1223, when Genghis Khan had begun to show the marks of age.

Kublai was one of the sons of Tului. He had grown up in the Mongol homeland, surrounded by a flock of cousins, most of them older than he was, and by many brothers. Mangu was the eldest of the sons of Tului, and then came Kublai, and after him Hulagu and Arik-buga. There were half-brothers besides, since Tului had several wives.

Young Kublai scarcely knew his father, for Tului was forever off doing battle. He had never laid eyes on his celebrated uncles Juchi and Ogodai and Chagadai, either. As for Genghis Khan, the head of the family, he was only a myth, a being of almost fantastic power who spent all his time campaigning in the land of the sunset, far to the west. Kublai was raised by his mother, Syurkuk Teni, the favorite wife of Tului. She had to be mother and father to him both, as every Mongol mother had to be, for the men were always at war.

Syurkuk Teni had been born in the Kerait tribe, long allied to the Mongols. The Mongols had no real religious beliefs, worshiping after their fashion the eternal blue sky and the spirits of nature. But the Keraits had been converted to Christianity by missionaries out of China, hundreds of years before. They were not Christians of the sort found in Europe, who were Catholics and obeyed the Pope. The Keraits belonged to the Nestorian sect, and had never heard of the Pope. They had their own rituals and prayers, quite different from anything in the Catholic faith, but they believed in Jesus Christ, who had died upon the Cross. The children of Syurkuk Teni heard the story of Jesus from their Christian mother, and Kublai in particular showed great interest.

But a Mongol boy's real love was for battle and hunting, not for talk of religion. So it was an exciting day for Kublai when Genghis Khan returned from the wars at last to rest for a while in his home territories.

All the grandsons he had never seen before were pushed forward to greet him. Kublai stood out from the others. He had been spoiled just a little by Syurkuk Teni, who wanted him to know more luxury than the Mongols were accustomed to. She had given him robes of Chinese satin to wear, and had decked him in the soft fur of the white fox. Kublai had eaten well, and he was plump, not hard like his cousins. His eyes were brown, and so was his hair.

"How dark he is," Genghis Khan murmured, when he first saw Tului's second son.

Plump or not, Kublai had to learn to hunt like any Mongol boy. Genghis Khan at nine years old had already been a skilled horseman. But this was a different generation, and Kublai at nine had not yet gone on his first hunt. Genghis took Kublai and his younger brother Hulagu with him into the forest. Kublai shot a hare, and Hulagu slew a stag. Genghis smiled at their success. It was the custom, when a Mongol boy had made his first kill at hunting, for an older man to rub the flesh and fat of the slaughtered animal on the boy's fingers, to speed his arrows thereafter. Genghis performed the rite for his two small grandsons. Hulagu, who one day would be the terror of the Near East, gripped Genghis' hands and would not let go. The Great Khan laughed and remarked, "You see how my offspring overpower my hands."

Then it was Kublai's turn. Genghis rubbed the grease on his middle finger. Glancing at the other Mongol leaders, Genghis suddenly declared, "The words of this boy Kublai are full of wisdom. Heed them well—heed them, all of you."

After that, Kublai was called Kublai Sechen, Kublai the

Wise. He was marked among the grandsons by Genghis' statement. And later the Great Khan said to his sons, "If you are ever in doubt what to do, ask this boy Kublai. One day he will sit in my seat, and bring you good fortune such as you have had in my time."

But the time of Genghis Khan was drawing to a close, and the time of Ogodai Khan was coming. Kublai was thirteen when his grandfather died, in 1227. Syurkuk Teni, his ambitious mother, hoped that her husband Tului would be chosen Great Khan at the khuriltai that had been called, and Kublai himself dreamed that his father would sit on Genghis' throne. But it could not be. Genghis himself had named Ogodai. Syurkuk Teni had to swallow her disappointment.

In her tent she spoke in low tones to her sons, telling them of her ambitions for them. Mangu, the eldest, was strong and silent, like his uncle Chagadai, and he could be a great leader one day. Hulagu was fiery and fierce, like his father Tului. But Kublai took after his mother. He enjoyed the luxuries of Cathay with which Syurkuk Teni decked her tent—the hangings of silk sewn with pearls, and the gleaming silver braziers in which incense burned. He asked many questions, and hungered to learn everything. Kublai the Wise, Genghis had called him. Syurkuk Teni was proud and amused at that. "I do not think thy words are always so wise," she told Kublai. "But *he* said they were, and what he has said is so."

Two scholars came to live among the sons of Tului. One was a Uighur merchant who knew the secrets of profit and loss. The other was Chinese, a man with a brush and a supply of ink, who could cover silk with mysterious symbols, and then make words rise from the marks he had made. Kublai learned how to read and write. Genghis Khan had not needed such skills. Tului could not read. But Kublai Sechen, Syurkuk Teni decided, would know the art of words.

The time for the khuriltai of 1227 arrived. From here and there came the Golden Family, so that Ogodai could be elected Great Khan. The meeting was held, as Genghis had commanded, in the ancestral Mongol homeland, now Tului's country. "He who remains in a distant place and does not come," Genghis had said, "will be like a stone fallen into deep water, or an arrow shot among reeds. He will disappear."

Tului was the host, then. Kublai watched his father make the preparations for the khuriltai. Tului seemed bitter and moody, for he felt destiny had passed him by. Syurkuk Teni, too, found it hard to contain her sorrow; another woman's husband would be Great Khan, and that grieved her. But Tului and his wife were outwardly gracious and cheerful as they welcomed the Mongols from the far-flung domains.

From the edge of the Russian steppes, three thousand miles away, came Batu, Juchi's son. He was Kublai's cousin, but much older than Kublai, full-grown and a great khan. From the southwest came Chagadai, nicknamed the Wild Horse, with camels and yaks carrying the baggage of his many followers. From conquered Khitai came Ogodai, the heir to the throne. At his side rode his chief wife, Turakina, full of pride because her husband was to be Genghis' successor. She was a big, powerful woman with a man's strength and a man's booming voice. Only Ogodai found her beautiful.

Tului was a generous host. He slaughtered sheep by the thousand, so that his relatives might feast. He opened the casks of *khumiss* and let the liquor flow freely. The Mongols laughed and sang, wrestled, raced, told tales of battle. After pleasure came the business of the khuriltai. Ogodai was now to be elected.

But Ogodai hesitated. He felt that he was too simple, too open a man to rule over all the empire. Let Tului have the throne, he said. Tului, though he burned with ambition, remembered the words of Genghis. Ogodai was to rule. The three brothers conferred. The debate dragged on and on. It might have lasted forever, but for Yeh-lu Ch'u-ts'ai, the wise Khitai minister who had been Genghis Khan's chief adviser. He knew that Ogodai was the proper successor, and that this delay was harmful.

The minister went to Chagadai. "Prince, you are the eldest. Unless you bow first to the new Great Khan, who else will dare to proclaim him?"

Chagadai held back no longer. He went to Ogodai and knelt before him. Tului did the same. Then the brothers seized Ogodai roughly by the arms, and dragged him to the throne, forcing him down on it.

"Ogodai, you are Great Khan," Chagadai shouted.

It was done. The power had passed to the second generation, and after two years of doubt, while the clans were gathering and debating, the throne was no longer vacant. Fifteen-year-old Kublai was among those who declared their devotion to Ogodai Khan. And Syurkuk Teni, who had never given up hope that the throne would somehow come to Tului, powdered her cheeks and donned her finest robes and went forth to congratulate her sister-in-law Turakina.

Ogodai was great of heart but slow of wit, and he depended on others to do his thinking for him. But he was true to the plan of Genghis Khan. The conquest of the world would continue, and the *yasas* would be upheld. Chagadai, who of all the brothers was closest to the old nomad spirit, saw to that. Whenever Ogodai's easygoing nature led him away from Genghis' ways, Chagadai reminded him of the right path. He was the enforcer of the law. Once Chagadai enforced it even against himself. When they were both drunk one day, he challenged Ogodai to a race. Over the prairie they galloped, and Chagadai won. Ogodai laughed and pounded his brother on the back and told him he was a magnificent horseman.

But when his mind was clear again, Chagadai realized what he had done. He had beaten the Great Khan in a contest—a sign of disrespect, of defiance. The next morning Chagadai came before his brother, who was sleepy and befuddled with drink.

"I have sinned against the Great Khan," Chagadai declared. "I must be punished. Judge me and issue your decree. Beat me with cudgels, or put me to death."

"Don't be a fool," Ogodai replied. "You are my brother."

But Chagadai stubbornly insisted on punishment. So Ogodai had him bow before the tent entrance, and present nine times nine horses as atonement, and then he issued his pardon. Not until then was Chagadai satisfied.

Though Ogodai was a simple man, his wife Turakina was complex and haughty. She objected to living in tents, even though they now were hung with silk. She urged Ogodai to build a palace, such as lesser kings than he lived in. But he was a nomad, a tent-dweller, and to him it was a crime against the nomad nature to settle down like a shopkeeper. To please her, though, he caused the first Mongol city to be built—Karakorum, near the Orqon River in western Mongolia. Juvaini's history of the Mongols declares that a great palace was constructed there, and a throne for Ogodai with three flights of steps. All the utensils were of gold and silver studded with jewels. Twice a year Ogodai would come there to hold court for a month at a time, but he was always restless and uncomfortable amid such splendor.

Shortly the Mongol troops were on the march once more. Soon Ogodai was hurling his army against what was left of the Chin Dynasty that controlled Khitai. Down into China rode the Mongol hordes. The Chin were well protected; after Genghis had driven them out of most of their territory, they had taken refuge south of the Yellow River. Natural fortifications shielded them on three sides: the Yellow River in the north, mountains in the west, the broad ocean in the east. Their cities were great and strong. Kaifeng, the capital, was forty miles around, and behind its sturdy walls lived four million people.

Genghis Khan had laid down a plan for attacking the Chin. They could not, he said, be defeated from the north or west. It was impossible for the Mongol armies to cross the Yellow River without being massacred by Chin defenders, or to get through the mountainous, fortified zones of the west. Nor could the Mongols, having no navy, attack by sea from the east. The only route into Chin territory was the one that was unexpected because it was so roundabout—through its soft southern underbelly.

Southern China was still ruled by native Chinese Emperors, the Sung Dynasty. Once the Sung had had possession of all of China, but they had lost control of the northern region when the Khitan barbarians invaded it. When the Jurchen-Chin Dynasty arose, more Sung territory fell into barbarian hands. For the Mongols to defeat the Chin, they would have to march through Sung-held China. But the Sung wanted nothing more than to see their old enemies, the Chin, overthrown. The Sung Emperor was glad to cooperate by letting the Mongols march through his domain on their way to do battle against Chin.

Ogodai launched a pincer movement in 1231. Aided by a brilliant general named Subotai, he led one army through Khitai to the Yellow River and attacked the northern frontiers of the Chin kingdom. Meanwhile Tului, with thirty thousand veteran soldiers, set out on a huge detour around the western end of China and down into the southwestern part of the Sung territory. Then the pincers closed. Caught between the two armies, the Chin were annihilated. The survivors took refuge behind the walls of Kaifeng, and a long siege began. The Mongols could be patient. Sooner or later, they would starve the enemy out.

It was the summer of 1232. Ogodai, a man of the north, was not accustomed to China's heat. He left Subotai in charge of the siege operation, and returned to his own land, taking Tului with him. Hardly had the Great Khan passed through the Great Wall that was the boundary between China and Mongolia when he fell ill. Fever blazed in him. The medicine men danced and sang and washed his body with wine and milk to cleanse him of the demons of disease, but Ogodai's skin burned and burned, and he sank toward death.

Tului, watching his brother suffer, cried out to the

spirits that infested Ogodai's body. "Let him live," he said, "and take me in his place." Ogodai recovered. The jubilant Mongols continued their northern trek. But just as they neared their home encampment, Tului sickened, and death carried him away in a few days.

News came to Syurkuk Teni that her husband was dead. Ogodai hurried to her side to console her, and Chagadai came from his domain in Central Asia. Kublai and his brothers, so suddenly fatherless, stood silent in their mother's tent.

It was not the custom for a widowed Mongol woman to remain a widow for long. When the time of mourning was over, Ogodai drew Syurkuk Teni aside and asked if she would marry his eldest son, Kuyuk. Many women would have leaped at the opportunity, for it was generally thought that Kuyuk would be Great Khan when Ogodai died. But Syurkuk Teni tactfully refused to marry Kuyuk or anyone else. She told Ogodai that she wanted simply to bring up her children in a proper way, and guide them to manhood, without giving herself to a new husband.

Ogodai accepted her wishes. He granted her control of all of Tului's lands—the Mongol heartland—to govern until they could be handed on to one of her four sons. Syurkuk Teni had never lost sight of her ambition. Now she could never see Tului become Great Khan, but perhaps she would live to see a child of hers on the throne of Genghis.

The war in China was going well under Subotai's direction during this time of Mongol sorrow. Chinese engineers sent by the Sung Emperor were aiding the Mongols in laying siege to the walled cities of the Chin. The Chin Emperor, with defeat staring him in the face, wrote to the Sung: "The Mongols have taken Hsi-Hsia and forty kingdoms. After the Chin will come the turn of the Sung. You do evil in aiding them." But the Sung, interested only in seeing the Chin swept away, paid no notice. And in 1234 the Chin Emperor took his own life, and his dynasty came to an end.

China now was equally divided, under Mongol rule in the north, Sung in the south. For the time being the Mongols had no plans to attack the Sung. The hot, swampy south was not tempting to them. And they had to pause and digest this huge new conquest before they went further. The minister Yeh-lu Ch'u-ts'ai was of great help here. He understood the Chinese and how they should be governed. The Mongols, though they were irresistible in war, still had little idea of how to rule over subjects in peace. China, with its many millions of people, baffled them. Ogodai took refuge in drinking, but Yeh-lu Ch'u-ts'ai set up a system of government that kept China from collapsing into chaos under Mongol control.

In 1235, Ogodai called a new khuriltai to discuss the next stage of Mongol expansion. After a long debate, it was decided to send out three armies. One would go deep into China, to sound out the possibilities of a conquest of the Sung. A second would venture toward northern India. But the main body of the Mongol strength would head due west as far as it could go—all the way into the unknown land of Europe that lay somewhere beyond the chilly plains belonging to Batu Khan.

Ogodai himself, who was getting old and loved his *khumiss* too much, would stay home in Karakorum. His son Kuyuk would go in his place on the western march. Two sons of Chagadai would also go, and Mangu, the older brother of Kublai. So there would be many of Genghis Khan's grandsons in the army of invasion. And Batu, the oldest grandson of all, would be its commander, with the veteran general Subotai beside him.

Kublai had taken no part in the great events of the past few years, and even now, when he had passed the age of twenty, he remained home when the army departed. It was the doing of Syurkuk Teni, who had plans for him that did not include his going off to war. She had sent one son, Mangu, to conquer Europe. That was sufficient. Kublai would stay back, continuing his studies, becoming a man of ideas instead of a man of war. There were warriors galore in the Golden Family, but not many thinkers.

Kublai had taken his first wife by this time. She was Jamui of the Konkurat tribe, a slender, delicate girl of great beauty. At least, Kublai thought she was beautiful, though some of his Mongol cousins privately felt that Jamui was too pale, too slim, too fragile-looking to be attractive. She had Chinese blood in her veins, which accounted for her looks. She was not flat-nosed and stocky like true women of the north. And Kublai, who loved all things Chinese for their elegance and grace, preferred her to the coarser girls of his own breed.

Nor was he content to live in a tent of felt. His house was Chinese in style, with tiled floors and beams of cedar. Genghis Khan might have sneered to see it. It was no house for a hard-riding Mongol, he might have said. But Genghis was dead, and the Mongols were changing as the ways of civilization came to them, and Kublai was changing more than any of the others.

There came to Kublai a new Chinese tutor, selected by Syurkuk Teni and Yeh-lu Ch'u-ts'ai. He was a quiet, solemn little man, deeply learned in many fields. Yao Chow was his name, and he was not entirely pleased with his new pupil. Kublai had a quick mind, yes, and knew a great deal. But he did not apply himself diligently to his studies. He was just a trifle lazy, perhaps, and enjoyed the pleasures of the feast, and spent too much time in the forests with his hunting falcons, and in his house with his pretty young wife.

"It is necessary for you to learn the principles of government," Yao Chow told Kublai.

The prince smiled. "I can manage as I am," he said.

Yao Chow disagreed. Kublai had much to learn. "It might just be," the tutor said, "that you will rule the world."

Kublai was startled at that. Many grandsons of Genghis Khan stood between him and the highest power. He settled down to study, all the same. And while he discussed with Yao Chow the proper conduct for a ruler of men, the Mongol hordes drew ever closer to Europe.

The army had set out in the summer of 1236. It moved unhurriedly westward, gathering strength from tribe after tribe as it continued along. In time it reached the territory of Batu Khan, and he welcomed his imperial cousins gladly and stuffed them with food and drink.

Batu had always been a little apart from the rest of his family, because he was Juchi's son, and Juchi might not have been truly the son of Genghis Khan. Batu felt the stain of doubt upon his ancestry. He had kept away from his cousins, off in the western steppes, living majestically on the banks of the Volga as the head of the branch of the family known as the Golden Horde. Now he found himself in command of this vast force. He was ill at ease, wondering if his cousins would really obey the son of Juchi. But Subotai was at his side, one of the last survivors of Genghis Khan's officers, and Subotai would maintain loyalty among the khans, Batu knew.

Subotai was the real strategist of the invasion. He divided the troops and sent Mangu off to deal with the wild Kipchak Turks. The Kipchaks melted away as Mangu approached. Meanwhile, when snow was falling late in 1237, Subotai led his own men northwest toward the large Russian cities. They fell one by one.

Batu went on ahead toward Europe, conquering city
after city until he grew weary of spring rains and turned
back to rejoin the main force. By the summer of 1238 the
Mongols were at the Black Sea, where they made contact
with another Mongol army that had invaded Persia four
years earlier. Again and again Subotai divided his forces,
so Mangu and Batu and Ogodai's son Kuyuk all had their
share of victories.

There were rivalries, all the same. Kuyuk was especially
embittered. He was the son of the Great Khan and was
generally regarded as the heir to the throne. But on this
expedition he was put in the shade by his cousin Batu, who
was older and more powerful. Kuyuk and Batu quarreled
so noisily that word of it got all the way back to Karakorum, where Ogodai now lay ill. The Great Khan sent an
angry message to the front lines, warning his son Kuyuk
not to be so headstrong, and telling Chagadai's two sons,
who also disliked Batu, to hold their peace. Just to keep
Batu in line, however, Ogodai added a deflating comment
for his eldest nephew: "As for you, do not boast so much
of your victories. They were gained by Subotai."

The disputes did not slow the Mongol advance. By 1240,
most of Russia was under their heel, and now they proceeded toward Western Europe. The finest soldiers of the
Christian nations were helpless before these barbarians.
The Mongols split again, a northern army smashing
through Poland and Germany, a southern army under

Batu and Subotai slicing into Hungary. Where would it end, the people of Europe wondered? Would the Mongols simply ride on and on, into France and Spain and Scandinavia, and then swarm across the Channel to overwhelm England, and go boiling into the sea to conquer whatever nations might lie in the west? It appeared that way. The Mongols were everywhere at once, and no army could stand before them. It seemed that millions upon millions of them had come pouring forth. An English chronicler wrote that "the detestable people of Satan, to wit, an infinite number of Tartars, broke forth from their mountain-compassed and rock-defended region, like devils loosed out of Hell . . . and like grasshoppers covering the face of the earth, spoiling the eastern confines with fire and sword, ruining cities, cutting up woods, rooting up vineyards, killing people both of city and country. . . ."

All the world would belong to the descendants of Genghis Khan. Europe was at Subotai's mercy. Chagadai was ravaging Persia and the Near East. Mongols had invaded Korea and were menacing Sung China.

Then, as though a switch had been thrown, the Mongol drive came to a sudden halt. The yellow-skinned horsemen who held the world by the throat turned round, called off their invasion, and headed for home. It was almost impossible for Europe to believe that the Mongols had relented, just when they were at the point of total victory. It was like a miracle.

What had happened was the death of Ogodai Khan at Karakorum. Couriers flying like arrows on the wind had sped across the world to Subotai's camp, reaching him in February 1242. Ogodai had died on December 11. In two and a half months, through winter snows, the word was brought to Subotai five thousand miles away, and went out from him to all the Mongol chieftains. The war must cease, Subotai declared—for a Great Khan was dead, and by the *yasas* it was necessary to return at once to the ancestral lands, and choose at a khuriltai the next Mongol monarch.

Batu objected. The war was going well, and he had no wish to interrupt it. Certainly he did not care to trek across the world to Karakorum to watch one of his cousins elected Great Khan. He knew that he had no chance himself, though he was now the oldest of the grandsons.

Subotai insisted, though, that Batu obey the *yasas*. The armies were called back. So that Europe would know that this was no retreat, but rather a voluntary withdrawal, the Mongols carried away loot as they passed eastward. "We are called away," they declared, "and we spare you war."

When the Mongols reached Batu's camp on the banks of the Volga, where his twenty-six wives awaited him, the master of the Golden Horde informed Subotai that he was going no farther. Batu was willing to let his cousins decide the matter of the successor to Ogodai without him. Subotai reminded Batu of the commands of Genghis: "The great ancestor said that those who do not appear at the gathering of the blood kin will be like arrows shot into reeds. They will disappear."

Batu agreed to go to Karakorum shortly. He was troubled with gout, he said—a painful affliction of the joints that was common among the descendants of Genghis Khan. Subotai left him and continued on to Karakorum. Then came a messenger from Batu: his gout was worse, and he was not coming to the khuriltai after all.

It was held without him.

Selecting the new Great Khan was a complicated matter. When Genghis died, there had been only the three sons to consider. But now there were many contenders for the throne—not only the grandsons of Genghis but some great-grandsons, too. Karakorum soon was buzzing with political intrigues as the various candidates jockeyed for power.

Ogodai, just before his death, had named his favorite grandson Shiramun to succeed him. It was not a popular choice. Ogodai's widow Turakina, in particular, opposed it. She wanted her son Kuyuk to succeed—not young Shiramun, who was descended from Ogodai by one of his other wives.

"Shall a grandson be chosen," Turakina asked, "while a son lives?"

Turakina, that powerful, bull-voiced woman, was in a

position of authority. By Mongol tradition the first wife of a dead Khan served as regent herself until the new Khan could be elected. So when Ogodai succumbed, Turakina took command of the Mongol empire. In this she was backed by her brother-in-law Chagadai, who had always been the guardian of the *yasas*. Chagadai, old and weak with illness, could not be named Great Khan himself. But he supported Turakina when she took control. She set aside the naming of young Shiramun as Great Khan. She was determined that the khuriltai would choose Kuyuk.

Syurkuk Teni, Kublai's mother, had her own candidate: her eldest son Mangu. He had distinguished himself valiantly in the war against Europe, while the sickly Kuyuk had done little. Syurkuk Teni felt that her son should be Great Khan. But Kuyuk was of the house of Ogodai, and many Mongols believed that the throne should pass to Ogodai's son. Syurkuk Teni soon realized that she did not have the power to put Mangu on the throne, so long as Turakina was determined to see Kuyuk become the Great Khan. Once more she bided her time and concealed her ambitions, as she had done when Ogodai was elected in preference to her husband Tului.

Not until 1245, more than three years after Ogodai's death, was the khuriltai finally held. The return from Europe had been slow, and several times the khuriltai had been postponed in the hope that Batu's sore foot would heal. But at last it became obvious that Batu would never come, and the khuriltai took place without further delay.

"No one," declares a chronicler, John of Plano Carpini, "had ever beheld such a gathering before."

Two thousand white tents were pitched by the shore of the Blue Lake, a hallowed Mongol meeting-place. Princes of many lands sent ambassadors, or came themselves, ready to pay homage to the new Great Khan after his election. Turks and Russians, Chinese and Arabs, lamas from Tibet and merchants from Samarkand, all rubbed elbows at this enormous assemblage in the Mongolian homeland. And, of course, at the center of everything were the tents of the Golden Family. Chagadai, last of Genghis' sons, had died the year before, but the grandsons and great-grandsons were many in number by now. Kublai was past thirty, still solemn and shrewd and very much different in personality from his rowdy brothers and cousins. When the feasting began, Kublai drank his share and sang and danced with the others, but behind his dark eyes his calculating mind was looking forward to a time when he would be something more than just a royal prince of a minor line. This was the great moment of Ogodai's family, Kublai knew— but time might bring many changes.

Kuyuk kept apart from the feasting. He was a reserved, self-contained man whose coldly majestic bearing made up for his lack of physical strength. No one could remember having seen Kuyuk laugh. Even his smile was a chilling thing. He had few friends, and surrounded himself with a bodyguard so that no one might have direct conversation with him. Within his frail body dwelled the spirit of a fiercely arrogant prince.

Hearty, good-natured Ogodai had disliked Kuyuk, and had tried to pass over him to give the throne to Shiramun. But Turakina chose otherwise. The khuriltai met only to ratify her decision, and Kuyuk became the third Great Khan of the Mongols in the spring of 1246.

His reign was short, as many had suspected it would be. Illness burned in him, making his eyes glow and his flesh waste away. He drenched himself in wine to ease his pain. Though many expected him to be dominated by Turakina, he quickly showed his independence. He put to death a slave-woman named Fatima who was thought to have a sinister influence on his mother, and executed also a sly minister named Abd ar-Rahman whom Turakina had entrusted with great power. Kuyuk intended to be his own master. His wife, Ogul Gaimish, stood beside Kuyuk, aiding him and lending him her own almost demonic strength.

Kuyuk feared the power of his cousins. He could not take action against the sons of Tului, for they were popular among the Mongols, particularly strong Mangu. But he meant to check the strength of Batu, whom he hated.

Batu had mocked him when they fought together against Europe. Batu had insolently refused to come to the khuriltai that was to elect Kuyuk. In theory, Batu was Kuyuk's vassal, bound to obey the word of the Great Khan. But actually Batu was far away in Russia, living in glittering splendor, practically a Great Khan himself. He did as he pleased, and Kuyuk detested him for it.

So Kuyuk called the Mongol army together and led it westward, toward the dominion of Batu. The horsemen plodded through the whirling sands of the desert, a long line stretching as far as eye could see. Kuyuk simply said that he was renewing the war against Europe. But before he could reach Europe he would have to pass through Batu's territory. The royal cousins would meet face to face —and one of them would be compelled to give way.

Batu was not worried. He could command six hundred thousand men, an army bigger even than Kuyuk's. And he would be on his own ground. He had been warned by Syurkuk Teni that Kuyuk intended to bring him to submission, but Batu was confident of his own strength.

War between the grandsons of Genghis Khan seemed inevitable.

Kuyuk's army halted at the edge of the desert, with the snow-capped mountains of the west in front of them. Batu marched east and made camp at the mouth of the Imil River, by the side of the Lake of the Eagles, and waited for Kuyuk to reach him. Why did the Great Khan's army halt? Batu grew impatient and uneasy as the days passed and the face-to-face confrontation did not occur.

Then came a courier from the east, riding with furious speed into Batu's camp with news that Batu had not dared to hope for.

"The Great Khan is dead of his illness," the messenger declared. Kuyuk's widow, Ogul Gaimish, was now the regent. Aided by her mother-in-law, old Turakina, she intended to rule until a new Great Khan was chosen. And the new Great Khan, the two women planned, would be the boy Shiramun, who had been bypassed in favor of Kuyuk. Kuyuk had reigned only two years; now, in 1248, Shiramun was still young, and Ogul Gaimish knew that he would be a puppet she could easily control from behind the scenes.

Ogul Gaimish courteously invited Batu to the Mongol camp to discuss the situation. Batu brushed the invitation aside. "My foot pains me," he reported. "I cannot ride."

But the gout was just an excuse. The oldest and most powerful of Genghis Khan's grandsons had no wish to ride meekly to the camp of his enemies. He, not they, would shape the future of the Mongol dynasty.

To Batu came a pair of visitors: Mangu and his brother Kublai. They had been sent by their mother to do a bit of political negotiating. Batu greeted them warmly. Kublai was virtually a stranger to him, but Batu respected his reputation for shrewdness. As for Mangu, he and Batu were old friends of the battlefield; they had fought side by side in Europe. The two young princes exchanged their views with Batu, and Batu liked what he heard.

Batu sent a message to Ogul Gaimish at the Mongol camp. Mangu and Kublai, he said, were already with him. Why not have the other grandsons journey to Batu's camp as well, and hold a khuriltai to pick the next Great Khan?

Ogul Gaimish and Turakina were dismayed. The last thing they wanted was to let Batu hold the khuriltai in his own country. They pointed out that by tradition the meeting must take place in the Mongol homeland. Batu would not care to make such a journey, so they would be able to control the election just as they had controlled the last one.

At this point Syurkuk Teni stepped in. She had waited nineteen years to make her move. "Batu is the lord of the grandsons," she exclaimed. "Who has the right to turn away from his word at this time?"

Syurkuk Teni was popular among many of the Mongols, who hated the haughty Turakina and feared the devilish Ogul Gaimish. Batu supported her, and so did the sons of Chagadai. There would be an immediate election. Turakina and Ogul Gaimish saw that they had been defeated. Syurkuk Teni had maneuvered into a powerful position.

Turakina and Ogul could do nothing but withdraw,

taking the body of Kuyuk back to Karakorum for burial. Their only representatives at the khuriltai were a few old soldiers loyal to Ogodai. The Mongols gathered in Batu's camp, but it was not a true khuriltai, for none of the men of Ogodai's family were present.

Batu and Mangu remained silent, letting the supporters of the house of Ogodai speak first. The old men set forth their reasons for keeping the throne in the family of Ogodai. Long ago, they said, they had pledged to give their support to Ogodai's descendants. They felt bound by the will of the second Great Khan, and did not want to let the throne go to a different branch of the family.

When they were finished, Kublai rose to speak.

"As you have said, so have we done," he remarked. "But the descendants of Ogodai were the first to go against the will of Ogodai. They raised Kuyuk to the throne, when Ogodai himself had named the boy Shiramun to follow him."

The chieftains backing Ogodai's family were abashed at this. But at least in bypassing Shiramun they had kept the title in Ogodai's line. Let Shiramun be named Great Khan now, they argued.

An old general who had fought in the army of Tului rose to object. "He is a child. The Great Khan must be a man," he declared. He nominated Batu for the throne, as the eldest of the princes.

Batu, though, did not want the honor. He preferred to

keep to his own domain in the west. And he knew that because of his clouded ancestry he would never win the full support of all the Mongols. So, in his meeting with Mangu and Kublai, Batu had agreed to step aside in Mangu's favor.

He spoke now, declining the throne and speaking of Mangu's bravery in battle, his nobility of character, his general popularity. He said that Mangu should have been elected in 1246, but for the scheming of Turakina and Ogul Gaimish, who put the sickly, spiteful Kuyuk on the throne. Now that injustice could be undone. Batu noted that Mangu, as a grandson of Genghis Khan, was a generation closer to the great ancestor than young Shiramun.

And now Kublai spoke again, in favor of his brother. His words swayed many. Had not Genghis himself once said "If you are ever in doubt what to do, ask this boy Kublai"? Choosing his words craftily, Kublai wove a net of argument around the listening Mongols. When he took his seat, the issue was settled.

Mangu would be Great Khan. At last the throne had passed to the house of Tului. A messenger departed to carry the joyous news to Syurkuk Teni. Batu smiled over his triumph, for he had been the architect of Mangu's victory. And Kublai, who had spoken so well at the meeting, looked toward the snowy mountains and saw his own future taking shape in an attractive way.

His brother Mangu would rule all the Mongols. Kublai would no longer be simply another grandson of Genghis.

He would be the Great Khan's most trusted adviser, his closest companion.

And, Kublai knew, a time would come when Mangu Khan would be no more, and then the Mongols might look to him as their leader. It had seemed impossible not so long ago, but now the shape of tomorrow was different.

"It might just be," Kublai's tutor Yao Chow had said, "that you will rule the world."

Kublai had laughed at that prophecy. But he laughed at it no longer.

FOUR · *A Stately Pleasure-Dome*

THE HIGHEST power of the Mongol world was in Mangu's hands. But he had been elected irregularly, chosen by a hastily assembled and one-sided gathering of soldiers in an armed camp far from the traditional Mongol homeland. Now he returned to the capital of Karakorum as Great Khan. Before he could feel that the title was really his, though, it had to be confirmed by a real khuriltai at which every branch of the family was represented.

The messengers went out to all the Mongol princes. But the house of Ogodai, sulking because its candidate had been set aside, refused to come. And the family of Chagadai also turned down the invitations. Though Chagadai's sons had no quarrel with Mangu, they felt that he had seized power improperly, violating the *yasas* of Genghis Khan.

Chagadai had always been the one most loyal to the old traditions, and his sons took after him in that respect.

The Mongol world was in a state of suspended animation. Without a Great Khan accepted by all, no action could be taken. The war in Europe, halted so abruptly in 1242, had not been resumed seven years later. What would become of Genghis' command to carry Mongol rule to the ends of the earth? Would the great empire collapse while the grandchildren of the conqueror quarreled over politics?

Syurkuk Teni, worried by the delay, wrote to Batu in Russia. "For two years we have sought to seat Mangu on the throne," she said, "yet the children of Kuyuk and Chagadai have not come."

"Set him on the throne," Batu answered, "and take the head from any living being who turns aside from the *yasa*."

A second time Mangu Khan sent his messengers to his hostile cousins. He reminded them that by their absence from the khuriltai they were themselves in defiance of the laws of Genghis Khan, and that the further advance of the Mongols would remain stalled until they ceased their stubbornness.

His words had great effect. The Golden Family set out from all parts of the far-flung realm. The date for Mangu's coronation was set by the astrologers for July 1, 1251. Juvaini's history of the Mongols tells us that on that day "the clouds had piled up, and the rains poured down, and the face of the sun was enclosed behind a veil of vapor and a screen of mist," and at the hour appointed for the ceremony it was so dark that the astrologers could not use their instruments to measure the height of the sun. But then, as the chosen moment arrived, the clouds parted and the sun appeared, and "the world was adorned with light and brightness, and the face of the earth emptied of shadow and darkness."

Mangu seated himself on his throne, with his brothers about him: Kublai closest by, with Hulagu and Arik-buga flanking them, and then the sons of Tului by wives other than Syurkuk Teni. Batu had been unable to come, but he sent in his place his brother Bereke, who also limped with the family gout. As the sullen members of the families of Ogodai and Chagadai arrived, they took their places, and the feasting began in a tent that Juvaini declares was "constructed of cloths of splendid texture," decorated with embroidery so beautiful it "appeared as a sky with the lights of the stars shining as lanterns, or as a garden wherein flowers and blossom were scattered like pearls. The floor of the tent, covered with carpets of all kinds in all varieties of color, seemed to be a meadow full of every sort of fragrant herb."

Juvaini's account adds that "they feasted and reveled for a week with care and malice banished far from the courtyard of their breasts. And every day in accordance with the dress of the World-Emperor they would don garments of a different color and quaff cups and goblets. And the daily ration of drink and food was 2000 wagonloads of *khumiss* and wine, 300 horses or oxen, and 3000 sheep."

Some had come not to revel but to slay. Conspirators of the house of Ogodai planned to wait until Mangu and his supporters were drunk, and then to fall upon them with knives. But the plot was discovered. The baggage of certain officers was searched and found to contain concealed weapons. Mangu Khan wished to be merciful to the conspirators, but his advisers convinced him that the safety of the entire empire depended on rooting out these traitors. To wish to take the life of the Great Khan was unthinkable treason.

So all those who had plotted against Mangu were put to death. The ringleaders were Ogul Gaimish and the mother of Shiramun—old Turakina had died—and the two women were taken before the Great Khan. Mangu asked them to swear allegiance to him. They refused. Syurkuk Teni, eager to see her enemies destroyed, showed no mercy. She persuaded Mangu to execute them. And so the widow of Kuyuk Khan was flung into a lake to drown, as was the mother of Shiramun.

The purge grew wider. In the closing months of 1251 everyone who had opposed the election of Mangu was hunted down and slain. Through all the vast realm of the Mongols, the cousins and nephews of the Great Khan were found and taken and killed, until the house of Ogodai was nearly wiped out. One of the few who escaped was young Shiramun. Kublai had a liking for the boy, and asked that his life be spared. Another who went unharmed was Kaidu, like Shiramun a grandson of Ogodai. Kaidu had been one of the heroes of the campaign in Europe ten years before, and Mangu could not bring himself to take the life of such a brave warrior—an act of mercy which would create grave problems for Kublai in the years to come.

When the purge was complete, the power of Mangu Khan was unquestioned. Syurkuk Teni had lived to see the sons of Tului in control of the empire Genghis had created. Of course, there was still Batu in the west, and no one pretended that he was under Mangu's thumb. But Batu and Mangu were good friends and agreed on all policies. Mangu once declared, "There are two eyes in a man's head, but although there are two, there is but one field of vision. What one eye sees, the other sees also. So is it with me and Batu."

In her hour of glory, Syurkuk Teni sickened and died. She was laid to rest beside Tului, not far from the grave of Genghis Khan, in the secret Mongol burial place somewhere in the north. "She was the wisest woman in the world," wrote the Persian historian Rashid-ad-Din about 1300. "She watched over her children until the time when the empire came, by her skillful management, to the hands of Mangu." But she had also driven a wedge through the

Golden Family with her ambitions. The old tribal customs had been disregarded, and Mangu had come to power through force, not through the unanimous consent of the descendants of Genghis. Syurkuk's son Kublai would continue the retreat from the Mongol traditions of old.

Now, though, it was Mangu who ruled. Though he was not the clever, educated man his brother Kublai was, he knew the importance of learning. He surrounded himself with wise men, philosophers, and religious teachers. All religions were of equal interest to him, and he often took part in the debates these scholars held. He valued science, too. When he sent his brother Hulagu to invade the Moslem world, Mangu gave him special instructions to find the mathematician Nasr-ed-Din and bring him to Karakorum to build an astronomical observatory. Mangu collected officials from many nations to staff his government—Persians, Uighurs, Tibetans, Chinese, and others. A strong man and a capable one, he had learned well from his mother how to rule an empire.

World dominion was Mangu's goal, because it had been the goal of Genghis Khan. He intended to send his soldiers to the ends of the world, until "there shall be only one ruler on earth as there is only one God in Heaven." But Mangu was not altogether sure why such a conquest should be carried out, though he was willing to obey his grandfather's desire and undertake it. He hoped that the purpose behind Genghis' plan would reveal itself when the plan was fulfilled. In a letter to the King of France setting forth his goal of conquest, Mangu expressed some of this uncertainty: "When, by the power of the Eternal God, the whole world from sunrise to sunset has been unified in happiness and in peace, then it will become plain what we shall have to do."

The Mongols were eager to return to their wars. For a full decade they had been occupied with their own family quarrels. Now Mangu prepared to put armies in the field once more.

He would not invade Europe. That was Batu's privilege. Batu was already raiding the nations of Europe again, sending one army toward the Baltic, another into Serbia and Bulgaria, as he retraced the victorious march of 1240 and 1241. Mangu looked toward Asia for his triumphs. In 1253, the Mongols resumed their war against the world.

Mangu let his three brothers share command of the forces. Arik-buga, the youngest, was given control of the home guard that defended Mongolia. This was traditional; his father Tului, also a youngest son, had had the same responsibility. Hulagu, the second youngest, was sent into the Near East to smash the Moslem world. Kublai drew the assignment of finishing the conquest of China. Other Mongol armies marched against Korea and India.

Hulagu was the most successful. His army rolled westward like a mighty machine, heading for a troubled part of the world where many powers contended. In Asia Minor there were Turks of the Seljuk tribe; in Syria and Egypt the rulers were of Arab stock; the Persians were of still another ancestry. They were all Moslems, worshipers of Allah, but they were forever locked in combat with one another and with the Christian Crusaders who had invaded the Near East a century and a half before. Hulagu blazed through Persia and on into Iraq. He followed the River Tigris to Baghdad and destroyed the most important center of the Moslem world; then he headed onward toward Syria, with Egypt as his ultimate goal. His troops knew only victory as they moved from city to city.

Kublai had never been the warrior Hulagu was. He had seen his first military action when he was only thirteen, in the last year of Genghis Khan's life, but he had no real taste for battle. Mangu and Hulagu loved to be in the thick of things, shedding enemy blood and roaring hymns of violence, but not Kublai. He had stayed home on the greatest of all Mongol expeditions, the one that made Europe tremble. Kublai was more comfortable in the pleasures of his home and in the delights of the hunt than he was on the field of battle. And now Mangu had asked him to do what no one had ever accomplished since the dawn of time: to conquer China.

Northern China, the part the Mongols knew as Khitai, had been conquered many times by nomad invaders in the last thousand years. The Great Wall, though it stretched nearly two thousand miles along China's northern frontier, had been of little use in keeping back the wild horsemen of Mongolia. But southern China, with its torrid jungles and many rivers, had never been successfully invaded. Its rulers were always men of Chinese descent.

The Sung Dynasty, which had come to power in the year 960, still ruled in southern China. The Sung Emperors were generally weak and foolish, given to the love of poetry and wine rather than to the arts of government, but China's natural defenses protected their land: the ocean to the east, the mountains of Tibet to the west, the impassable jungles of the tropics to the south, the wide rivers to the north. A line of fortresses also guarded the northern frontier. The Mongols had ruled in Khitai since 1234, but their occasional efforts to overthrow the Sung had been half-hearted and met with no success.

Kublai, when he set out for China in 1253, welcomed the task ahead of him. He loved China and its luxuries and relished the idea of dwelling there, surrounded by fine porcelain vases, elegant painted scrolls, clever Chinese poets, and lovely Chinese women. Yao Chow, Kublai's old tutor, recognized this weakness in him. He saw that Kublai was in danger of being swallowed up by the ways of China, losing the Mongol strength of purpose that was the source of his authority. So when Kublai descended into Mongol-occupied Khitai, Yao Chow warned him against getting enmeshed in Chinese culture. "The Middle Kingdom [China] is most to be desired of all," he said. "It holds the seed of culture and true richness. But, my prince, you must try to separate yourself from the people of the Middle Kingdom. It is wiser for you to assume only military government, and leave the administration to lesser officials."

Kublai listened attentively. But the lure of things Chinese was too strong for him. He began to plan a palace for himself, to be built at a place called Keibung, on a fertile plain near a lovely river. Keibung was north of the Great Wall, and so was not truly within China. But it was close enough so that Kublai could feel the influence of the Chinese. He planned to make his palace at Keibung his summer capital. During the winter he would live at another capital city to the south, within China proper. In time, the conquered Chinese would call Kublai's city at Keibung *Shang-tu*, "the Upper Court." Shang-tu would become *Xanadu* in the writings of medieval Europeans who visited China, and it would bear that name in Coleridge's famous poem written six hundred years later. But the "stately pleasure-dome" at Xanadu was still only a dream when Kublai passed that way in 1253. Sung China had to be dealt with before he could start to build capitals.

Kublai knew that China could never be conquered in a direct thrust from the north. A chain of fortresses protected the border, and millions of Chinese existed to man those fortresses. The Mongols could hurl themselves at China for hundreds of years without making a dent in that huge population. The attack had to come from an unexpected direction or it would inevitably fail.

From which direction, though? Kublai looked to the west. The mountains of Tibet rose like icy fangs, stabbing into the sky. Could an army possibly cross the frosty Tibetan plateau and come down into China from the southwest? Kublai conferred with Mangu, and Mangu advised him to try. He gave Kublai his most trusted general, Uriangkatai, the son of famed Subotai, and placed a hundred thousand men at his command.

No army had ever taken the Tibetan route before. It was an incredible journey, through mountain passes so high that it was a struggle to fill the lungs with air, and across ice-bound valleys where the dreadful cold froze men's blood in their veins. Mountain tribesmen resisted the Mongols every step of the way. Kublai subdued them and forced them to guide him through this land of unending winter. A thousand miles the Mongols marched in the mountain world, until they left the white wasteland behind them and came down into the region the Chinese called Yunnan, which meant "south of the clouds."

A kingdom called Nan-chao existed here. Yunnan had never been part of China, and the Nan-chao people had turned back all attempts by the Chinese to conquer them. The Mongol leaders paused to plan their strategy. They were still frostbitten from their unbelievable march through the mountains. Here the weather was quite different, and even harder to bear—for this was tropical country where sweat ran like rivers under Mongol armor and strange insects buzzed through the muggy air, bringing discomfort and disease. The Mongols who had come safely through the terrible cold now began to die by the thousands in Yunnan's smothering heat.

Kublai sent envoys to the king of the Nan-chao, demanding surrender. The king put the Mongol envoys to death. Kublai attacked, and drove the king into hiding. But the war against Nan-chao was just beginning. Walled cities defied the Mongols.

It was not pleasant to carry on a war in such a climate. The Mongols were northerners who had little liking for heat. Kublai, watching his men die of disease, did not want to risk open combat with his fever-weakened troops. Old Yao Chow told him a tale of a legendary Chinese general who had once captured an enemy town without killing anyone, and Kublai decided to try the same method. "What you have been telling me is a fable," Kublai exclaimed, "but tomorrow I shall actually do it."

He had silk banners inscribed with the slogan *On pain of death, do not kill!* Then he approached the gates of Tali, the capital city of Nan-chao. The Mongols forced their way in, shouting their slogan. Gradually the men of Tali realized that if they did not resist, they would not be harmed. The city fell with scarcely any loss of life.

But Kublai had had enough of the hothouse climate of the southern lands. He left Uriangkatai in charge and returned to the more comfortable weather of Khitai to supervise the construction of his palace at Shang-tu. Uriangkatai was a general of the old school who would not try to conquer a city by waving banners at it. He completed the conquest of Yunnan, though by the end of the summer only twenty thousand of the original hundred thousand Mongol soldiers still were alive.

During his campaign, Uriangkatai encountered a kind of warfare no Mongol army had ever faced before. Armored elephants thundered out of the steaming wilderness toward the Mongols. The Mongol horses panicked as these monstrous beasts of war advanced on them. For once the hard-riding horsemen of the north were compelled to do battle on foot. They dismounted and shot flaming arrows at the elephants. Enraged by the pain of their burns, the elephants went berserk and swung around, trampling through their own army and creating havoc. Then the Mongols charged, taking advantage of the enemy's confusion to carry the day.

Sung China's southwestern frontier was now in Mongol hands. But Kublai did not take the next step—a simultaneous attack on the Sung domain from two fronts at once. Instead, he remained at Shang-tu without attempting to carry the war any farther. He concentrated on winning the friendship of the Chinese subjects of Mongol-held Khitai. Kublai distributed seed, oxen, and cows to them, to help them re-establish their economy after the years of hardship they had suffered. He chose native Chinese officials to carry out the day-by-day routine of government, and that increased his popularity even more. The vast Sung realm south of the River Han remained independent, however, and to the Mongols in the north it began to seem as though Kublai did not intend to continue the attack.

At Karakorum Kublai's enemies whispered insulting things. Many Mongols had never liked him; they thought he was too soft, too clever, too well educated, too Chinese in his tastes. They had believed that he would certainly perish in the hardships of his Tibetan march, but Kublai had fooled them. Nor had the summer heat of Yunnan laid him low. But the whisperers said that Kublai had had his fill of warfare after enduring the cold and the heat of his campaign. They spread rumors that he no longer meant to take the field, but instead would live at ease in his new palace in Khitai. And why was he coddling the Chinese that way, giving them seed and cattle? The tough Mongols of the homeland could not understand treating conquered peoples so kindly.

Mangu Khan, who had remained at Karakorum while his brothers Hulagu and Kublai waged war in distant lands, was troubled by what he heard. On the one hand, he heard only news of victory from Hulagu, rampaging through the Near East. On the other came these strange stories of Kublai's inactivity in China. He was angered by Kublai's failure to behave as a Mongol of the line of Genghis should.

A Mongol named Alamdar went to China bearing an imperial message from Mangu. Kublai was ordered to turn control of occupied China over to Alamdar at once and to return to Karakorum to explain his actions to his brother.

Kublai would not disobey Mangu's command. He permitted Alamdar to take charge and made ready to journey north. But Alamdar's first measures outraged Kublai. He executed many of Kublai's Chinese officials, saying that it was wrong to entrust to such men the administration of China. He began an investigation of all that Kublai had done, as though he suspected high treason.

It was rare for Kublai the Wise to fly into a blind rage, but his wits deserted him now. He gathered his officers and laid plans to overthrow Alamdar. Kublai was ready to make war against Mangu, if necessary, rather than let his work in China be undone. It would have been disastrous for the Mongols if war had broken out between the brothers.

Yao Chow, the old Chinese tutor, calmed the enraged Kublai. "You are your brother's first subject," he said, "and must set an example of obedience. Send your wives and children to your brother. Then go yourself, to tell him that all you possess, and even your life, belong to him."

Kublai's temper cooled and he recognized the wisdom of the old man's words. He went humbly to Karakorum and came before Mangu. Four years had passed since the brothers had seen one another. There had been many misunderstandings, and each had uttered harsh words against the other. But now that they were together, Kublai and

Mangu could hold no hatreds. Mangu threw his arms about his brother and called for *khumiss*, and they sat down to talk about their disagreements.

It was no difficult matter to patch up the quarrel. Kublai explained what he had been trying to do in China; he said that he felt it was wiser to try to win the friendship of the millions of Chinese than to attempt to rule over such a multitude by force of arms. And Mangu saw that Kublai was right; the Mongols were outnumbered hundreds of times over by the Chinese, and it might be better to rule by kindness than through terror in such a situation. Genghis Khan would not have agreed, but Genghis had been gone for thirty years, and conditions were different now.

But Mangu reminded his brother of one of Genghis' guiding principles: "Whenever you begin a war, whatever happens you must fight it to a finish." Had Kublai delayed in the conquest of Sung? No matter. The war would now proceed—and Mangu himself would take part.

"Our fathers and lords who were kings before us did a great work," Mangu Khan declared. "Each one of them seized a land and made his name shine before all men. Now I shall go in person to the wars, and make for the south of China."

Late in 1257, Mangu journeyed to the grave of Genghis Khan and offered sacrifices, asking for his grandfather's blessing in the coming campaign. Then he left his youngest brother, Arik-buga, in charge of the home pastures and rode off to do battle in China.

The assault would be a three-pronged one. Mangu would enter China from the northwest, Kublai from the northeast, and Uriangkatai would come up out of Yunnan to pierce the southwestern frontier. Not even the huge manpower resources of Sung China could meet so many challenges at once.

Kublai set out from Honan province, which he had ruled for years. He conquered all the country north of the Yangtze River, then forced his way across the Yangtze and laid siege to the great city of Wu-chang. Those who said Kublai Khan was no warrior were forced to eat their words, for Kublai led his men as bravely as any Mongol chieftain had ever done.

Uriangkatai, who had waited none too patiently in humid Yunnan for the past three years, erupted across China with the same ferocious impact. He marched northeastward until he was in the heart of China, then turned due north, taking many key cities, and headed for the plains south of the Yangtze. The plan was to make contact with Kublai's army, cutting Sung China in half.

Mangu's progress was equally swift. He crossed the province known as Szechuan and besieged the major fortress of Ho-chow, perhaps the most powerful of all the

Sung fortifications. Ho-chow offered sturdy resistance, though, and the siege dragged on into the summer months of 1259.

Kublai, meanwhile, had the center of the Sung domain at his mercy. The Sung prime minister, Chia Ssu-tao, led an enormous Chinese army against the Mongols, but when he reached the Yangtze he saw that it was hopeless to try to fight against Kublai's small but awesomely fearless force. Instead he secretly opened peace negotiations with Kublai. The Mongol prince, who had never cared to waste human life if he could accomplish his purposes peacefully, listened with interest to Chia Ssu-tao's proposals. The Chinese minister offered to pay an annual tribute in gold and silk to the Mongols, to surrender the northern frontier of Sung territory to them, and to recognize Mongol supremacy in the rest of China.

While Kublai and Chia Ssu-tao bickered over the terms of the treaty, stunning news reached the Mongol camp. An epidemic of dysentery had swept through the army that was besieging Ho-chow. Many Mongols had perished of the disease—among them the Great Khan Mangu. The dead Khan's soldiers had called off the siege and were getting ready to return to Mongolia.

Kublai was shaken by his brother's death. Mangu had still been a young man in his full strength. He might have had twenty years of power ahead of him. Now he was gone. And when Kublai recovered from the shock of his loss, he realized that if he moved swiftly the throne would be his. Quickly Kublai accepted the offer of submission that the Chinese minister made. But he left no Mongol army of occupation. Actually, the Mongols were withdrawing before their conquest of China was complete. Kublai made haste to reach his own provinces in the north.

The arrow-messengers rode to every corner of the Mongol empire with the news. Word reached the Golden Horde in Russia, but Batu was not there to learn that the man he had helped to make Great Khan was dead. Batu himself had been carried off by illness in 1254. His son Sartak had died soon after—some said he had been poisoned—and now the brother of Batu, Bereke Khan, ruled on the banks of the Volga. Bereke, the first descendant of Genghis Khan to be converted to the religion of Mohammed, was a man of independent mind. It mattered little to him who the Great Khan might be. He would pay lip service to the man while ruling with imperial splendor in the west, heedless of anything that might happen at Karakorum. So Bereke, like Batu before him, remained in his own territory instead of taking part in any Mongolian khuriltai.

Hulagu, the conqueror of the Near East, made plans to go home as soon as he learned that his brother was dead. The cheerful, fearless Hulagu had greatly annoyed his Moslem cousin Bereke by demolishing most of the nations of that faith. Persia, Iraq, and much of Syria were his. Son of a Christian mother and married to a Christian woman, Hulagu was hailed as a savior by the Christians of the Near East, and he enjoyed their friendship. Christian knights, Crusaders, marched with Hulagu's army. He planned to take Jerusalem away from the Moslems and give it to his Christian friends, and then to go into Egypt to shatter the last enemy stronghold. But in the midst of these plans came the courier from Karakorum. The tie of blood called Hulagu homeward.

He was not eager to go. Here in the wealthy Near East he had an empire worthy of his valor. If he left it now to attend a khuriltai, it might be years before he returned. Bereke, who hungered for new lands, might seize Hulagu's conquests—for Bereke certainly would not go to the khuriltai. Hulagu's own generals urged him to continue the war. "The Great Khan who is now dead," they said, "gave command to destroy Egypt." Why return? Tradition ordered it, yes—but was it reasonable to abandon a successful war simply to place Kublai on the throne? Kublai could make himself Great Khan without Hulagu's help, the generals argued.

Hulagu wavered. But tradition drew him. He announced his departure, and left a garrison of troops to hold his conquered territories until he returned.

But Hulagu had got no farther east than Persia when a courier overtook him with unbelievable news. An Egyptian army had attacked the Mongol garrison and wiped it

out! Never since the great days of Genghis Khan had
Mongols tasted defeat—but now a savage general named
Baibars had made himself Sultan of Egypt and had given
the Mongols their first setback since the beginning of the
century. Hulagu was appalled. He could not go to a
khuriltai in the face of such a crisis. He turned back at once
—and found that Baibars had allied himself with Bereke
Khan. Hulagu was confronted by a doubly powerful army
that blocked him from completing his conquest. He had
no choice but to wage war against Baibars and Bereke. The
forces were equally balanced, however, and a stalemate
resulted.

For the first time, there was actual civil war between
grandsons of Genghis Khan. Mongol soldiers clashed with
Mongol soldiers. The stalemated war dragged on for years.
Hulagu had lost his chance to destroy the Moslem world
when he turned back to go to the khuriltai. And, until his
death by poisoning in 1264, he found himself embroiled in
conflict with his cousin Bereke.

A word from the Great Khan at Karakorum, reminding
them both of the ideals of Genghis Khan, might have
halted the war. But there was no Great Khan at Karakorum. The Mongols were at odds in the east as well as in
the west.

The death of Mangu in 1259 left only two contenders
for the title of Great Khan: Kublai and his youngest
brother, Arik-buga. Bereke and Hulagu were too deeply

occupied with their own enterprises in far parts of the world. Another possible candidate was Kaidu, the grandson of Ogodai, but he belonged to a branch of the family that now had little political strength.

In Kublai's own view of the situation, there was no doubt of what had to be done: he saw himself as the logical successor to Mangu Khan. Kublai was now the oldest and most powerful living grandson of Genghis, and he had gained experience both in battle and as the ruler of occupied China.

There were many Mongols, though, who were wholeheartedly opposed to Kublai. These were the ones who still kept to their nomad ways, living in tents, scorning all luxuries. They were tough Asiatic pagans who disliked Kublai because he had adopted so many Chinese habits. How could this man claim to occupy the throne of Genghis Khan, they asked? He was no true Mongol, this Kublai. He was soft, scholarly, comfort-loving. Could he ride day and night for weeks, in the Mongol manner? Could he endure hunger and thirst? Could he inspire terror?

Kublai's enemies were clustered at the Mongol capital of Karakorum. They included many descendants of Ogodai and Chagadai, and regarded themselves as the only real keepers of the *yasas* of Genghis Khan. Before Kublai could arrive for a khuriltai, these men nominated Arik-buga and recognized him as Great Khan. Once more the messengers went forth, bearing the news of the election.

Pledges of support for Arik-buga came from many sides.

The three sons of Mangu swore allegiance to him. Kaidu and Bereke announced that they backed his claim. The widow of Mangu added her backing. All these powerful Mongols were uneasy about Kublai, who had turned so far away from nomad customs. Bereke had a second motive for backing Arik-buga. He knew that Kublai was certain to challenge the election and that civil war in Mongolia might follow. That was just what he wanted, for it would give him an opportunity in the confusion to carry on his own war against Hulagu.

Kublai Khan was still at Shang-tu when news came to him of his brother's election. In June 1260 he responded in his own way. He called a khuriltai at Shang-tu that was attended only by his own officers and by Chinese generals loyal to him. Solemnly they proclaimed him Great Khan.

The *yasas* had been ignored twice. Genghis had commanded that a Great Khan could be chosen only by a gathering of all the members of the family. Instead there had been two khuriltais, each representing part of the family. And now there were two Great Khans.

Kublai knew that the title would mean little without the allegiance of all the Mongols. He had the military might to enforce his claim. He marshaled his troops, battle-hardened veterans eager for a fight, and led them against the forces of the old-line Mongols. First Kublai attacked and defeated the army that had been Mangu's. Next he met and scattered the troops of Arik-buga in a decisive encounter. Then he surrounded Karakorum and starved the city into submission. Arik-buga escaped into the Gobi Desert. With a small force, he carried on guerrilla warfare for several years. Kublai made no real attempt to crush him, for he knew that Arik-buga could only be a nuisance now, not a dangerous enemy.

Arik-buga's raids continued until 1264. Then his army was cut off by Kublai's troops and all were taken prisoner. The dejected Arik-buga was brought before his brother, expecting to be slain. Kublai spared his life, but put to death all of Arik-buga's supporters. The opposition was crushed. Kublai was the lord of all the Mongols.

Hulagu, who had only a few months to live, sent his congratulations from Syria. Bereke, careful to stay on the winning side, despatched gifts to show his respect for Kublai. Only one diehard faction of Mongols refused to accept Kublai's rise to power. These were the rugged ones who clung to nomad ways, the descendants of Ogodai and Chagadai. They took refuge in the mountains of Central Asia. Their leader was the wily, fiercely independent Kaidu Khan, Ogodai's grandson. For the next forty years, Kaidu would be a thorn in Kublai's side, carrying on a permanent rebellion in the west.

Kublai did not immediately go after Kaidu, once Arik-buga was out of the picture. Rather, he returned to Shang-tu to take stock of his situation. He had no illusions about the way he had become Great Khan. It had been a triumph of force, a seizure of power that by traditional Mongol law had been highly illegal. Nevertheless it was done, and Kublai ruled. He knew that because of the shaky legality of his title he could never claim the allegiance of the outlying members of the Golden Family as Genghis or Ogodai had done. Many Mongols would always regard him with suspicion and coolness. The khans of the west, therefore, might swear allegiance to him, but their words would have little meaning, and they would heed his commands only when it pleased them to do so. The Mongol world was beginning to split into separate empires. In Russia, Bereke's Golden Horde was completely independent. In Persia ruled the son of Hulagu, who called himself the *Il-khan*, "lesser khan." In Central Asia there had emerged what was called the Chagadai Khanate, ruled by Kaidu. And Mongolia and much of China belonged to Kublai, the Great Khan.

As if to symbolize the changes that had occurred in the Mongol world, Kublai turned his back entirely on Karakorum and the rest of the ancestral homeland. He abandoned the desert city and took his court south, establishing his capital inside the Great Wall. He built a new city in China alongside the ruins of the old Chin capital of Yenching—where Peking stands today. The center of the Mongol world had shifted. Now Mongolia itself was only a desolate province, and Kublai Khan ruled from northern China.

FIVE · *The Fall of China*

THE YEAR 1265 saw Kublai firmly upon his throne. Mongolia was his, and half of China; Arik-buga was defeated; Hulagu's son Abaqa and Bereke's successor Mangu Timur recognized Kublai as Great Khan; the terrified Sung rulers of China waited for their inevitable downfall. Only Kaidu opposed Kublai, and Kaidu did not represent a serious threat.

Kublai had just passed his fiftieth birthday. In the Imperial Palace at Peking today is kept a portrait of the Great Khan painted by an unknown Chinese artist in that year. Kublai is dressed in Chinese style. His rounded face is firmly set, revealing energy, vigor, intelligence. His slanted eyes have the gleam of dignity and power. A drooping mustache nearly conceals his lips. On his chin there sprouts a tiny tuft of beard, a typical ornament of the Mongol sovereigns. It is the portrait of a strong and confident ruler who has emerged at last from the shadows of relatives and now sees years of greatness ahead.

His seat of power was Shang-tu, for the great capital city at the site of old Yenching had not yet been built when the portrait of 1265 was painted. Here, in his palace of fine marble, Kublai held court, listened to the information brought him by envoys from every part of his domain, and laid his plans for the completion of the conquest of Sung China. When affairs of state bored him, he could amuse himself by watching the performances of court magicians, who caused things to appear and disappear with great cleverness, or he could savor the pleasures of the hunt. Kublai's hunting park, encompassed by a wall sixteen miles around, was well stocked with game. Marco Polo gives us a surprising but accurate picture of the Great Khan at his sport: "Sometimes he rides through the park with a leopard behind him on his horse's crupper; and then if he sees any animal that takes his fancy, he slips his leopard at it, and the game when taken is made over to feed the hawks." Such trained hunting-leopards were employed by many Oriental monarchs.

Within this great park Kublai caused the construction of another palace, made entirely of cane. "It is gilt all over," according to Marco, "and most elaborately finished inside. . . . The roof, like the rest, is formed of canes, covered with a varnish so strong and excellent that no amount of rain will rot them. These canes are a good three palms in girth, and from 10 to 15 paces in length. . . . The construction of the palace is so devised that it can be taken down and put up again with great speed; and it can all be taken to pieces and removed whithersoever the Emperor may command. When erected, it is braced against mishaps from the wind by more than 200 cords of silk."

The finest Chinese craftsmen were kept busy designing and building these wonders for Kublai at Shang-tu—the marble palace, the palace of cane, a pavilion of ermine-lined leopard skins, courtyards and gardens and ponds. All this would have been strange and even distasteful to Genghis Khan. Two other buildings would have seemed stranger still to the old warlord. First, Kublai permitted the construction of a temple of Confucius in his park. Confucius, who had lived about 500 B.C., had been a wise adviser to early Chinese kings, and for hundreds of years the Chinese had worshiped him for his sagacity. Confucianism was not really a religion, but a way of life; it spoke not of gods and supernatural beings, simply of the responsibilities and obligations of a good citizen. Many of Kublai's Chinese subjects were Confucianists, and it was a sign of his religious tolerance that he allowed such a shrine to rise at Shang-tu.

The other unusual building was also Chinese, not Mongol, in nature. It was a palace in honor of Kublai's dead ancestors. The Chinese called such palaces *Tai-miao*, and built them to serve as memorials for each of the royal dynasties that had ruled their land. Kublai was not only the Mongol Great Khan, but also the Emperor of much of China, by right of conquest. So he gave his family a Chinese dynastic name, calling it the Yuan Dynasty, meaning "The First Beginning." And he followed Chinese fashion by erecting a *Tai-miao* for the previous members of his dynasty.

The custom was to give each Chinese Emperor an honorary title after his death. Kublai therefore awarded the four previous Great Khans such titles, naming Genghis *T'ai Tsu*, "Grand Ancestor." Ogodai, Kuyuk, and Mangu also received dynastic names. Memorial tablets were placed in the shrine to honor Yesukai, the father of Genghis, and also Juchi, Chagadai, and Tului. In this way Kublai retroactively turned the family of Genghis into a Chinese dynasty, which certainly would have astonished the founder of the line.

Though Kublai called himself Emperor of China, he knew that his title would not have full meaning until the rival Sung Dynasty of the south was obliterated. So once more he prepared to make war against the Sung. Between 1253 and 1259 Kublai had led the invasion in person. He had nearly defeated the Sung in 1259, when the death of Mangu had cut short his campaign. Kublai had been forced to withdraw hastily, though not before compelling the Chinese prime minister Chia Ssu-tao to sign a treaty of submission. As soon as the Mongols were gone, however, Chia violated the treaty. He massacred a small garrison of Mongol troops that had been left on the Sung side of the Yangtze, and boasted to his Emperor of this great victory, even claiming that his valor was the reason for Kublai's retreat!

Some nine years passed, and Sung China remained in peace, rebuilding its fortifications and hoping that Kublai would stay away forever. Once he had disposed of Arik-buga, Kublai sent ambassadors to the Sung to discuss Chia's breach of the treaty. The Chinese, with the boldness of desperation, slew the envoys. Kublai needed no further provocation to renew the war.

The Great Khan himself did not head the Mongol army this time. Though he was fond of China, Kublai did not care for the great heat of the south, with the diseases it fostered. The death of Mangu in a tropical epidemic had been a sobering reminder of the dangers of venturing into that climate. Besides, Kublai was no longer young, and even in his youth he had not cared for battle. Now he was heavy from feasting, and his indulgence in *khumiss* had given him the family curse—gout. His swollen, aching toes kept him in agony. The court physicians could do little for him, but Kublai tried every remedy. In 1267, he heard that boots made of the skin of a certain seal found in northern waters were helpful in such cases. A Mongol envoy journeyed to the court of the King of Korea, who was more than glad to be of service to his dangerously powerful neighbor. Seventeen seals were captured by Korean fishermen and the skins sent to Kublai. But his feet continued to ache.

The gouty Khan would not go to the wars, but he had gathered about him a group of generals he trusted like brothers. They would lead the war against the Sung.

A magnificent civilization was the prize of conquest. Sung China was famed for the beauty of its porcelains, the grace of its painted scrolls, the delicacy of its poetry. Nowhere else in the world were the arts so highly developed. The land was prosperous, too; there were half a dozen Sung cities with populations of more than a million, and the vessels of the large Sung navy plied every Asian waterway, bringing wondrous goods from foreign lands in exchange for Chinese silks and porcelains. From India and Africa came ivory, incense, camphor, pearls, crystal, agate, sandalwood, a wealth of jewels and spices and perfumes, carried by the giant ships called junks, with crews of several hundred men and sails so huge that one Chinese writer compared them to "great clouds in the sky."

The most splendid of the Sung cities was Quinsay, the modern Hangchow. Marco Polo, proud as he was of his native Venice, gasped in awe when he first beheld Quinsay about 1280 and called it "beyond dispute the finest and the noblest in the world." Like Venice it stood upon lagoons, crisscrossed by countless canals spanned by innumerable bridges. The main street ran from end to end of the city, a distance of many miles, with a great plaza every four miles. And within the city was a huge lake on which the citizens rode in gilded barges, so that they could, as Marco declares, "take in the whole city in its full beauty and grandeur, with its numberless palaces, temples, monasteries, and gardens, full of lofty trees, sloping to the shore."

The task of bringing all of this richness into the power of Kublai Khan was entrusted to a general named Bayan, who in his youth had fought under Hulagu in the west. About 1265, Hulagu sent him to Kublai as part of an embassy, and the Great Khan was so taken with Bayan's bearing and abilities that he kept him in his own service.

Bayan's name meant, in the Mongol language, "great" or "noble." But to the Chinese it had the same sound as the words *pei-yen*, meaning "having a hundred eyes." And an old Chinese legend foretold that a man with a hundred eyes would seize the empire and overthrow the dynasty. So when word reached China that Bayan was marching against the Sung, the superstitious Chinese cried out, "The hundred-eyed one is coming! We are doomed!" Terror sapped their strength—for who could hope for victory when all the astrologers said that the man with a hundred eyes would triumph over China?

Bayan was a superb general. Even the Chinese respected

him; one of their historians wrote, "He was endowed with a lofty genius, and possessed in the highest measure the art of handling great bodies of troops. When he marched against the Sung, he directed the movements of 200,000 men with as much ease and coolness as if there had been but one man under his orders. All his officers looked up to him with absolute trust, and obeyed him with entire submission. . . . He was never seen sad except when forced to shed blood, for he was sparing even of the blood of the enemy."

Kublai shared Bayan's feelings about bloodshed. This very unferocious Mongol ruler had always objected to unnecessary slaughter. He looked forward to a time when he would rule the conquered Chinese, knowing that the only way he could hold such a populous nation in check was by winning its affection, not its hatred.

Bayan moved south, storming fortress after fortress. Many cities, feeling that it was hopeless to resist, simply opened their gates to the Mongols. They trusted Bayan's promise that no civilians would be harmed, and Bayan kept that promise—unlike his Mongol forebears of fifty years before, who deliberately slaughtered whole populations in order to frighten other cities into surrender. Bayan depended on kindness instead of terror, a reverse psychological warfare that got good results.

Sometimes he had to give battle, of course. Then the Mongols fought fiercely, and each battle ended the same way: with the invaders in command and the Sung military officers committing suicide to avoid capture. Bayan thoughtfully gave these dead soldiers the proper Chinese funeral services, and that won him more support among the people he was invading. When plague broke out in the Chinese cities, Bayan sent Mongol physicians to treat the sick. He helped peasants to raise their crops in the fields trampled by soldiers.

The main invasion route led down the Han River to the place it met the Yangtze. Quinsay, the capital, was located at the joining of these two rivers. It was necessary for the Mongols to get control of the Han if they hoped to conquer Quinsay. But the heavily fortified twin cities, Hsiang-yang and Fan-ch'eng, blocked their advance. Bayan reached these cities in 1268 and began a siege, but they held out valiantly for year after year. Kublai grew impatient as the reports from the battlefront piled up with no sign of progress.

A Turkish general named Alihaiya told Kublai that the only way the two fortresses could be taken was by using heavy artillery: machines that could cast stones at their walls. The Mongols had used catapults and slings since the time of Genghis Khan; when Subotai invaded Chin China in 1232, he was equipped with engines that threw great boulders against the battlements of the city, and with machines to hurl firebrands over the walls. But these Mongol weapons were crude and unreliable. Alihaiya informed Kublai that better weapons were available from the West.

Powerful catapults called mangonels had been developed in Syria and Palestine during the fiercest days of the Crusades.

Kublai sent messengers to his nephew Abaqa, the Il-khan of Persia, asking for engineers. Abaqa supplied two capable men skilled in the art of designing the new catapults. They demonstrated their craft before Kublai at the Emperor's new capital city in northern China, and late in 1272 he sent them to aid in the siege of Fan-ch'eng.

They built engines of two kinds. The heavy catapults shot stones weighing up to 150 pounds against the city walls. They made a great noise as they operated, creating panic among the defenders. Such stone-throwing catapults were known to the Chinese as *pao*. Abaqa's engineers designed a second type, known as fire-*pao*, which shot flaming arrows great distances into the city. The people of Fan-ch'eng protected themselves by fashioning ropes of straw four inches thick and a dozen yards long. They strung these ropes across the roofs of the buildings and plastered them with clay. Nevertheless, the attack was successful. Fan-ch'eng soon surrendered, and a few weeks later its twin Hsiang-yang on the other bank of the river also yielded.

Now the gateway to inner China was open.

Kublai avidly followed the fortunes of his soldiers as they pressed ever southward. At home, many projects occupied him, the most ambitious being the construction of his Chinese capital, beginning in 1271.

The site of the city was just north of Yenching, the old

Khitai capital that Genghis had destroyed in 1215. It lay in the northeastern part of China and had never been used as a capital by any native Chinese dynasty; only the various barbarian invaders had chosen to rule from there, since it was convenient to their homelands in the north.

Kublai gave his new city the name of *Tai-tu*, "the Great Court." So it was known in Chinese, at any rate, but the Mongols called it *Khan-baliq*, "City of the Khan." When Marco Polo wrote his account of the city, he transformed Khan-baliq into *Cambaluc*, and that was the name by which it was generally known to Europeans of that day.

Cambaluc was a city worthy of its builder. Marco, who first saw it five or six years after Kublai founded it, wrote that "the city of Cambaluc hath such a multitude of houses, and such a vast population inside the walls and outside, that it seems quite past all possibility. There is a suburb outside each of the gates, which are twelve in number; and these suburbs are so great that they contain more people than the city itself. . . . In those suburbs lodge the foreign merchants and travellers, of whom there are always great numbers who have come to bring presents to the Emperor, or to sell articles at court, or because the city affords so good a market to attract traders."

The city was perfectly square, and Marco says it was six miles long on each side, all walled round with earthen walls of great height, topped by loopholed battlements. "The streets are so wide and straight," he wrote, "that you can see right along them from one gate to another. And up and down the city there are beautiful palaces and many great and fine houses in great number. All the plots of ground on which the houses are built are four-square, and laid out in straight lines. . . . Each square plot is encompassed by handsome streets for traffic; and thus the whole city is arranged in squares just like a chessboard, and disposed in a manner so perfect and masterly that it is impossible to give a description that would do it justice."

At the heart of the city was Kublai's own palace. "You must know that it is the greatest palace that ever was," declared the dazzled Marco. "It is enclosed all round by a great wall forming a square, each side of which is a mile in length; that is to say, the whole compass thereof is four miles." Watchtowers rose at the corners of this outer wall, manned by vigilant garrisons. Within was a second wall, also guarded by towers, and Kublai's palace proper occupied a courtyard adjoining this inner wall. "It has no upper story, but the basement is ten palms higher than the ground surrounding it, and the roof is surpassingly high. Flush with the floor of the palace, there is a marble wall, running all round, two paces wide. . . . The outer edge of the wall holds up a fine pillared balcony, that one can look out of. On each side of the palace is a great marble staircase, which leads from the ground to the top of the marble wall, by which one reaches the palace. The inside walls of the halls and rooms are all covered with gold and silver, and on them are painted beautiful pictures of ladies and knights and dragons and beasts and birds and divers other things. The ceiling is also made in such a way that one sees nothing else on it, but pictures and gold."

When we read the Venetian's description of Kublai's great hall, we understand why Europeans refused to believe that Marco Polo could possibly be telling the truth: "The hall of the palace is so large that it could easily dine 6000 people; and it is quite a marvel to see how many rooms there are besides. The building is altogether so vast, so rich and so beautiful, that no man on earth could design anything superior to it. The outside of the roof also is all colors with vermilion and yellow and green and blue and other hues, which are fixed with a varnish so fine and exquisite that they shine like crystal. . . ."

It was a far cry from the simple felt tent with which Genghis Khan had been satisfied. And amid the pomp and splendor of the court of Cambaluc, Kublai Khan listened with mounting pleasure to the bulletins from the Chinese front.

The war was going well. The fall of the twin Han River fortresses early in 1273 signaled the end of the Sung Dynasty. In 1274, the Sung Emperor Chao Ch'i died after a reign of nine years. He had been a weakling and a drunkard, scarcely able to lead his country in its time of peril. But in place of a poor leader there now was no real leader at all. The new Emperor was Chao Ch'i's three-year-old son, Chao Hsien. His mother, the Dowager Empress, served as the regent. As one city after another fell to Bayan's Mongols, the Empress and her son took refuge behind the walls of Lin-ngan. She sent an emissary to Bayan, asking, "Can you be so cruel as to make war against a little boy, and rob a helpless child of his realm?"

Bayan had studied Chinese history and was ready with an answer. In 960, when the Sung Dynasty was founded, its first Emperor had overthrown a weak dynasty called the Later Chou. The last Later Chou Emperor had been only a boy. So Bayan made the mocking reply, "Have you forgotten that the Emperor of the Chou, from whom your founder seized the empire, was also a child? Is it so strange that we do the same to you?"

The Empress retreated with her son to Quinsay, the capital. Bayan laid siege. Now she lost all hope, remembering the prophecy that a hundred-eyed one would destroy the dynasty. She invited Bayan into the city to discuss terms of surrender.

The gates of mighty Quinsay were opened wide, and the Mongol hordes rode proudly into the Chinese capital. Bayan approached the palace. The Empress asked him to enter and come before her, but the rough-hewn Mongol general, ill at ease among the delights of a Sung palace, refused, saying, "I do not know the proper ceremonial." The Empress and the boy-Emperor went to Bayan. Though her ministers had advised them to commit suicide, she preferred to throw herself on the mercies of the Mongol general.

Kublai had given orders that no one was to be harmed in Quinsay—particularly not the members of the royal family. Bayan was under instructions to maintain order and prevent his soldiers from pillaging the city. They were carefully to collect all works of art, books, and maps, and bring them to Kublai's court, along with the Emperor and his mother, who were to be given the best of treatment.

The Empress ordered her son to kneel and knock his head nine times against the floor in token of his submission to Bayan as the representative of Kublai Khan. "The Son of Heaven grants you life," she said. "It is fitting to render thanks to him."

The captive Emperor began the journey to Cambaluc in the third month of the year 1276, to take up life as Kublai's prisoner. Though treated well, he died a year later, at the age of six.

Sung China had fallen. But one pocket of resistance remained. Certain Sung ministers had fled from Quinsay toward the cities of the southeastern coast, taking with them the elder brother of the little Emperor. When Chao Hsien became a prisoner, they proclaimed eight-year-old Chao Shih the new Sung Emperor, and continued the war. The Mongols were compelled to send troops into the hot, swampy lowland country where their usual methods of battle were of little value. They forced the demoralized

Chinese to surrender, but at great loss to themselves. Kublai's generals were compelled to open the jails and draft twenty thousand Chinese prisoners into their army. The youthful Emperor and his ragged court wandered south along the coast, keeping just ahead of the Mongol advance. Only the city of Canton now remained to the Sung. The Mongols surrounded this large port, blockading it by sea. Here they were at a disadvantage, for they had scant experience at naval warfare. Chao Shih and his followers managed to escape by ship under cover of fog.

All through 1277, the Sung navy, or what was left of it, held the Mongols at bay, while the Emperor himself shifted from one coastal islet to another. The following year a typhoon shattered the Sung fleet, and Chao Shih himself died on the island of Kang-chou at the age of ten.

Most of the Chinese ministers were in favor of ending the hopeless war. But one royal prince remained, seven-year-old Chao Ping. A faction of diehard loyalists proclaimed him the new Emperor. With twenty thousand followers and a thousand ships, the last of the Sung monarchs entrenched himself on the offshore island of Yai-shan.

The Mongols surrounded Yai-shan and besieged it for a month. The defenders were stubborn and well fortified, but their food and fresh water began to give out. After a savage battle that lasted from sunrise to sunset, a Chinese minister named Lu Hsiu-fu decided that the only hope lay in breaking the Mongol blockade and escaping to another island. Under darkness the imperial Sung fleet set sail.

The Mongols closed in. Only sixteen Sung ships slipped through the net, including the flagship that bore Lu Hsiu-fu and the little Emperor. The Mongol fleet set out in pursuit, easily cutting off the bulky Chinese vessel. Lu Hsiu-fu ordered his wife and children to leap into the sea to avoid capture. Then he took the royal child in his arms.

"An Emperor of the Sung Dynasty chooses death rather than imprisonment," Lu Hsiu-fu cried, and plunged overboard, to be swallowed by the sea.

After three centuries, the Sung Dynasty was at its end. China had fallen. Kublai Khan, grandson of the fierce Genghis, was Emperor of China, the Son of Heaven, resplendent in his yellow robes as he mounted in triumph the famed Dragon Throne of the Middle Kingdom.

SIX · *Strangers from the West*

AMONG THOSE on hand at Cambaluc in 1279 to congratulate Kublai Khan in his moment of greatest glory were the Polos of Venice. We have already seen how it came to pass that Marco Polo journeyed to Cathay with his father and his uncle, arriving there in 1275 on the eve of the final Mongol conquest of China. Soon Marco, like many other foreigners, was finding a place for himself in the government of Kublai Khan. With a single family of Mongols ruling all of Asia from the Pacific to the shores of the Mediterranean, enforcing a general peace, it became possible for other Europeans to make the long trek to legendary Cathay, once they had heard the wonders Marco Polo had to relate.

But before any members of the Polo family had ever set foot in Mongol territory, there had been visitors from the West. The stories of these travelers are so extraordinary that they deserve retelling.

Contact between Europe and the great empires of Asia had always been an uncertain thing. The distances were too great, and the men of Europe had feared the perils of unknown seas. About a hundred years before Christ, there was a flourishing trade between Rome and China, but the exchange of Roman gold for Chinese silks was carried on by Persian middlemen, and there was never any direct commerce between the Middle Kingdom and Rome. When nomad barbarians from the north invaded China about A.D. 250, this trade broke down entirely. About 625 Christian missionaries of the Nestorian sect reached China and got a friendly welcome from the new T'ang Dynasty, but these men were from Syria and Armenia, not from Europe. And after the fall of the T'ang in 906, all links with the West were broken once again.

Arab merchants came by sea to do business in the Chinese ports when the Sung Dynasty emerged. Of Europeans there were none. Asia was a mysterious, virtually unknown world all through the early medieval period in Europe. In 1095 the great Christian holy war known as the Crusades brought Europeans to the shores of Syria, but the Crusaders showed no curiosity at all about what might lie farther to the east. Asia remained unvisited.

When Batu and Subotai and the Mongol hordes spilled out into Europe between 1236 and 1241, it was no longer possible for Europe to ignore Asia. For a few years it seemed that the nations of the West would become Mongol provinces. Then came the death of Ogodai Khan; the invaders withdrew to select their new ruler. There were no further Mongol invasions of Europe. The Christian world recovered from its fright and began to ask questions about these Mongols. Was it true, as some said, that they were Christians? Could it be possible to form an alliance with them? Rumor had it that the Mongols hated the Moslems—and so did the Europeans. A tempting possibility presented itself: an alliance between Christendom and the Mongol world, designed to destroy the worshipers of Mohammed.

Only three years after the withdrawal of Mongol troops from Europe, Pope Innocent IV decided to explore in a serious way the prospect of such an alliance. He chose a Franciscan monk named John of Plano Carpini to make an amazing journey into Mongolia as an ambassador to the Khan of the Golden Horde, Batu. Clad in his coarse brown robe, his head shaved, his feet bare but for sandals, Friar John mounted a donkey and set out with a single companion as an interpreter, bound for the Mongol realms.

No hardship dismayed him. By the spring of 1245, Friar John was jogging through the devastated regions of Poland and Bohemia. At the city of Krakow he presented himself to the duke, who provided him with an escort as far as the Russian city of Kiev. In February 1246 the friar passed into Mongol-held territory. At once, he wrote, "armed Tartars came rushing upon us in uncivil and horrible manner, but after making inquiries they accepted some food and immediately departed." With nothing to defend him but his letter from the Pope, Friar John moved unharmed through the Mongol lines and traveled down the Dnieper River, frozen by winter's grip, to the Black Sea, which was also covered with an icy sheet. There he reached the terrifying Batu Khan, who struck Friar John as "courteous enough unto his own men, and yet is he had in great awe by them; he is most cruel in fight, and exceedingly prudent in war."

Batu was greatly surprised that Friar John should have survived his lonely winter journey, and somewhat impressed by the monk's endurance. He listened with polite interest while Friar John explained that he was a messenger from "our lord the Pope, the father and lord of the Christians, going to the Tartar nation, to desire peace and friendship between the Tartars and the Christians." Friar John declared that the Pope wished the Mongols to embrace Christianity, if they were not already of that faith, and to cease their slaughter and repent of what they had done.

It seemed to Batu that his Mongol cousins would find the Italian friar a pleasant curiosity. So he replied amiably that he had no authority to decide matters of imperial policy; Friar John would have to take his message farther east. The khuriltai at which Kuyuk was about to be elected

Great Khan was then in session, and it was to Kuyuk that John would have to address himself.

On Easter Sunday, with two Mongols as guides, Friar John and his companion set out for the khuriltai. "We departed with many tears, not knowing whether we went to death or to life. And we were so feeble in body, that we were scarce able to ride." But they rode at a rugged pace, changing horses five times or more a day. John traveled with sharp eyes, and made a detailed and unusually accurate record of all he saw—the geography, the customs of the Mongols, local religious practices, and much else. Whatever he observed personally he saw well, though sometimes he was willing to accept at face value stories of a fantastic nature. Like every man of his day, Friar John believed that weird monsters lived in the remote parts of the world. Though he failed to see any monsters himself, he did put in his report to the Pope a secondhand tale of creatures "in the shape of men, which had each of them but one arm and one hand growing out of the midst of their breast, and but one foot. Two of them used to shoot in one bow, and they ran so swiftly that horses could not overtake them. They ran also upon that one foot by hopping and leaping, and being weary of such walking, they went upon their hand and their foot, turning themselves round, as it were in a circle."

Late in July, Friar John arrived at the khuriltai. He had ridden some three thousand miles from Batu's territory to reach it. "We saw a huge tent of fine white cloth pitched," he wrote, "which was, to our judgment, of so great quantity that more than 2000 men might stand within it. . . . And there were all the Tartar lords assembled, each one of them riding up and down with his followers over the hills and dales."

He looked with disapproval on the Mongols' love for *khumiss:* "At noon they began to drink mare's milk, and they kept on till evening, drinking amazing amounts. They invited us to drink with them, treating us with ale, as we did not drink mare's milk—but they compelled us to drink so much that we could by no means endure it."

Kuyuk appeared and "was greeted with a sound of music, and was saluted with beautiful rods tipped with scarlet wool. . . .They told us that four thousand envoys had come to him with gifts. Among the gifts were silk girdles wrought with stones, and a canopy covered with precious stones, and numbers of camels having trappings of brocaded cloth, with horses decked in leather or iron links. . . .We were asked what gifts we had to offer, but we were unable to present anything."

The entire gathering knelt before Kuyuk—all but Friar John, for the Mongol was no sovereign of his. The monk was brought before the newly elected Great Khan and offered his message. Kuyuk took it coolly. When asked if he were a Christian, the Khan replied, "God knows. And if the Pope also wishes to know he had better come and see."

Friar John was given to understand that the Mongols planned to conquer the world, and that only the death of Ogodai had interrupted their progress. Kuyuk dictated a chilling statement that John of Plano Carpini took down word for word in Latin. He explained how, "By the will of the Eternal Sky, all the earth from the rising to the setting sun has been given us. How could anyone go against the commands of the Sky? You ought to say now, sincerely, 'We will be your subjects, we will put our power at your service.' If you do otherwise, how can we know what will happen to you? Only the Sky will know."

It was no message of good cheer that Friar John brought with him out of the lair of the dreaded Mongols. But he had been treated well and fairly, and Turakina, the mother of the Great Khan, even gave him fox-skin robes to keep him warm on his homeward trip. He studied the Mongol leaders carefully—for he was, in fact, a spy—and took stock of the enemies of Christendom. He did not mention Kublai, though he probably saw him, and he said of Kublai's mother Syurkuk Teni that she was "the greatest lady among the Tartars and the most honored, except the mother of the Emperor, and more powerful than any subject save Batu."

In June 1247, Friar John and his companion appeared

before the city of Kiev, where "the citizens rejoiced over us, as over men that had been risen from death to life." A few months later they called upon the Pope in France and gave him Kuyuk's frosty letter with its grim declaration: "God has commanded my ancestors and myself to send our people to exterminate the wicked nations."

John of Plano Carpini had negotiated no alliance with these deadly foes of Christendom, but he had brought back much useful information, including the welcome news that while Kuyuk himself was no Christian, there were many influential Mongols who belonged to the Nestorian sect. And at least the Mongols seemed to despise the followers of Mohammed, so there was still hope for a league of Mongols and Christians against the Moslems.

A few months after Friar John's return, Kuyuk was dead. The promised extermination of the people of Europe did not occur. Mongol power passed to the noble Mangu, whose mother was Christian. Once more the rulers of Europe dreamed of winning the friendship of the Mongols —and once more a Franciscan friar made the immense journey to the tent of the Great Khan.

He was William of Rubruck, fat, jolly, inexhaustible. King Louis IX of France, a saintly man who had gone Crusading, sent him to the Mongols in 1253. King Louis had heard the tantalizing rumor that the leaders of the Mongols had become Christian—most notably Sartak, Batu's son. So off went Friar William to negotiate for

Mongol soldiers to aid in the Crusaders' attack on Egypt.

William's journey was not so startling as that of Friar John, because he was following the earlier man's route while John had simply plunged off into the unknown. It was equally taxing, though. He crossed the Black Sea to the Italian colony of Soldaia, where the elder Polos then resided. Then he proceeded inland, traveling with ox-drawn carts. "When I met Tartars for the first time," he wrote, "I thought myself entered into another age."

Shrewdly noting down everything he saw, Friar William toiled eastward until he came to Sartak's camp, where he was welcomed with customary Mongol hospitality. "Now as concerning Sartak, whether he believes in Christ or not, I know not," the friar reported. "He hath about him certain Nestorian priests, who pray upon their beads and sing their devotions." He was not impressed by these Asiatic Christians, though, commenting that they "know nothing. They say their offices, and have sacred books in Syrian, but they do not know the language and they are utterly depraved."

Sartak sent the friar along to his father Batu, whom William warned, "You shall not obtain the joys of heaven, unless you become a Christian." Batu treated Friar William to *khumiss* in a golden vessel and gave orders for him to be conveyed to Karakorum to present his letters to Mangu Khan. The Mongol guide assigned to the monk was unsure that Friar William would survive the trip. "Think well whether you will endure it," he said, "for the winter cold cracks trees and breaks rocks asunder."

Wrapped in a sheepskin jacket, socks of felt, and leather boots, Friar William endured the cold. Through all the thousands of miles of the journey he recorded penetrating observations on the customs of the tribes through whose territory he passed—Uighurs, Tanguts, Keraits, and others. He asked about the strange beings Friar John had heard of: "I was inquisitive of the monsters or monstrous men. . . .They told me they never saw any such, whereof we much wonder, whether it be true or not." In December 1253 the weary traveler arrived at Karakorum and came before Mangu Khan.

"The house was all coverd inside with a cloth of gold and there was a fire . . . in a grate in the center of the dwelling," wrote Friar William. "Mangu was seated on a couch and was dressed in a skin spotted and glossy, like a seal's skin." The Great Khan "appeared to me to be tipsy," and so was the interpreter, so the interview accomplished little. But a short time later the friar was granted a second audience with Mangu, and this time presented his letters and spoke briefly about Christianity.

Mangu, son of a Christian woman, examined William's cross "without seeming to worship it in any way." Then began a famous religious debate, as Buddhists and Moslems and Nestorian Christians and representatives of other faiths at Mangu's court put forth the advantages of their creeds.

Friar William took part, and found himself agreeing with the Nestorians and even the Moslems on one basic point—that there was only one God. He spoke intolerantly, however, and angered the easygoing Mongol audience, which accepted most religions with equal willingness.

At a later interview, Mangu himself declared his religious beliefs: "We Mongols believe that there is only one God, by whom we live and by whom we die, and we have an upright heart towards him."

"God grant you this," said Friar William, "for without this gift it cannot be."

Mangu went on, "As God hath given the hand many fingers, so he hath given many ways to men. God hath given the Scriptures to you Christians, and you keep them not. . . .To us he hath given soothsayers, and we do that which they bid us, and we live in peace."

Friar William asked permission to stay at the court and preach Catholicism. Mangu had had enough of the monk's narrow-minded views, though, and ordered him to leave. Mangu might well have been interested in peaceful contact with Europe, but William's lack of diplomatic tact irritated him into making belligerent threats. He gave the friar a letter for King Louis of France, foretelling a day when "the whole world shall be at one, in peace and rejoicing," and warned the princes of Europe to prepare themselves to submit to Mongol government or be destroyed. In the summer of 1254 Friar William departed from Karakorum, and the following year he reached Christendom, carrying the discouraging news that the Mongols were beyond all understanding—sympathetic to all religions, but subject to none, and following some divine plan from which they would not swerve.

By the time the next strangers from the West reached a Mongol Great Khan, there was no longer any fear of an invasion of Europe. The great plan of Genghis had miscarried, because of the conflicting ambitions of his grandsons. The Mongols of the Golden Horde made war against the Il-khans of Persia instead of resuming the assault against Europe. And the Great Khan Kublai, now on the throne, saw himself as a purely Asiatic monarch who was concerned only with conquering the lands that bordered on China.

These new visitors were Niccolo and Maffeo Polo. As we have seen, they set out for the camp of Bereke Khan in 1260 and found themselves cut off from Europe by the warfare between Bereke and Hulagu. Unable to return, they went forward instead and reached Kublai's court at Shang-tu in 1265, just after the Great Khan had defeated the forces of Arik-buga and taken supreme command.

The Polos were traveling privately, not as official ambassadors, so they did not attempt to establish any kind of political alliance between the Mongols and the European powers. It would have been a pointless thing to do, in any event, since the entire aspect of the Mongol world had changed since the days of Kuyuk and Mangu, and the divided people of Genghis Khan had ceased to issue ringing, insolent challenges against the West. As good Christians, however, the Polo brothers described their faith to Kublai, and found a willing listener—even, it seemed to them, a potential convert.

They did not realize that Kublai's interest in Christianity represented partly his general curiosity about the world and partly his shrewd political sense. The Great Khan, as he questioned the two Venetian merchants about the details of their religion, was eager to learn all he could about every sort of creed. At that stage in his reign, he was maintaining the traditional Mongol spirit of religious tolerance. At the court of Shang-tu could be found Buddhists, Confucianists, Taoists, Nestorians, Moslems, Tibetan Lamaists, and representatives of many idolatrous pagan sects of the Orient—and Kublai listened to them all.

The Great Khan saw religion as a political matter, though. He found himself the ruler of a vast domain containing men of many faiths. It would be easier to govern these people if he employed officials of their own religions. He himself had no religious preference, but he was willing to be friendly to all faiths where he saw it to his advantage as a monarch.

When Kublai asked the Polos to bring him "some hundred wise men learned in the law of Christ" to teach their faith in Asia, the brothers were certain that they had won the entire Mongol nation over to Christianity, but it was actually Kublai's political sharpness at work again. He recognized the usefulness of having able counselors and learned foreigners at his court. Already he had accepted the services of a number of Mohammedans, but he did not entirely trust them. It would be valuable to keep a corps of Catholic priests in his service as well, as a balancing check against the Moslems. Then, too, his conquest of Sung China was about to resume. Kublai had a good relationship with the Chinese officials of Khitai, who were accustomed to serving barbarian overlords. As he subjugated the south, however, he realized that the native Chinese civil servants would resent the Mongol yoke and quite likely would be treacherous and dangerous if he left them in office. Kublai wanted his hundred Catholic priests to help him govern Sung China after he conquered it—for there would be a definite shortage of trained administrators in his empire if he removed all the Chinese from power.

Still, the Polos deceived themselves into thinking that Kublai was going to become a Christian as soon as the hundred missionaries arrived. Kublai himself fostered this impression in a sly, teasing way. While Niccolo and Maffeo were at Shang-tu, the Great Khan learned that it was the Christian Easter holiday. Marco tells us:

"He summoned all the Christians, and bade them bring with them the Book of the Four Gospels. This he caused to be incensed many times with great ceremony, kissing it himself most devoutly, and desiring all the barons and lords who were present to do the same." The Polo brothers discovered that Kublai was in the habit of honoring the Christian Scriptures this way at Easter and Christmas—but that he also paid the same homage at the high festivals of the Moslems, Jews, and Buddhists of his realm.

One of the brothers asked Kublai why, and the Great Khan replied, "There are four prophets worshiped and revered by all the world: Jesus Christ, Mohammed, Moses, and Sakyamuni [Buddha]. I worship and pay respect to all four, and pray that he among them who is greatest in heaven in very truth may aid me." Then he quietly told the Polos that his private belief was that Christianity was the truest and best religion of all.

"If you hold our faith to be the best," replied the Venetians, "why do you not attach yourself to it, and become a Christian?"

Kublai offered a strange response. He indicated the Nestorian Christians at his court—his own mother's sect. "Why should I make myself a Christian?" he asked. "You see well enough that the Christians of these parts are so ignorant that they achieve nothing." Kublai pointed to the Tibetan lamas, the priests of a Buddhist offshoot that made much of magic and the supernatural. "These men can do anything they please," the Great Khan said. "When I sit at table the cups from the middle of the hall come to me full of wine or other liquor without being touched by anybody, and I drink from them. They can conjure up storms, causing them to pass in whatever direction they please, and can do many other marvels; while, as you know, their idols speak to them and predict the future. How can I dare become a Christian with such magicians at my court? They would use their black arts to bring about my death."

It is hard to imagine the crafty Kublai as really afraid of the Tibetan sorcerers at his court. Though there was an element of the primitive, barbaric Mongol in his personality, he was much too sophisticated a man to have much fear of magicians. More probably he was amusing himself at the Polos' expense. The brothers must have looked uneasily toward the sinister figures of the Tibetans.

Quickly the Great Khan held out new hope that he might become a Christian after all, despite the secret supernatural powers of the lamas. "Go to your Pope, and pray him to send me a hundred skilled in the law of Christ, who can rebuke these idolaters to their faces, and can say that they, too, can do such things, but do not wish to because they are done by the help of diabolic art and evil spirits. Let them control the idolaters so that they have not the power to do such things in their presence. When we see this, we shall denounce the idolaters and their religion; and so, I shall be baptized, and when I am baptized, all my barons and chiefs shall be baptized also, and their followers too, and so there will be more Christians here than there are in your part of the world!"

The Polos were greatly excited by the prospect of being the instruments of the conversion of the whole Mongol empire. When they returned to Christendom in 1269, they told their story to the authorities of the Church. We have seen that the new Pope, however, could spare only two priests, and these two lost heart before they got far on their journey. So no missionaries came to Shang-tu at all. Marco Polo innocently wrote, "If the Pope had sent men fit to preach our religion, the Great Khan would have turned Christian; for it is an undoubted fact that he greatly desired to do so."

Kublai must have been disappointed, too, when the Polos returned in 1275 without the promised hundred priests. He could have put those men to good use in his ever-expanding empire, which now included almost all of Sung China. The brothers had brought him someone of value nevertheless: young Marco, whose eyes were keen and whose brain was nimble, and whom he took into his service in place of the hundred priests who had not come.

The Great Khan was no longer tolerant of all religions as he had been ten years before, in any event. Kublai had fallen under the influence of a Tibetan lama named Phags-pa, and this devious, scheming sorcerer wielded a mysteriously powerful control over him. The Great Khan gave the lama many titles of honor: "King of the Great and Precious Law," "Imperial Mentor," "Creator of the Empire." He officiated as high priest of the court, and the somber rituals of Lamaism pushed the Christian, Moslem, and Buddhist services into the shadows. Kublai accepted Phags-pa's opinions on many political and intellectual matters, as well as religious ones. The lama devised a new alphabet to replace the Uighur Turk script that Genghis Khan had borrowed for his Mongols; but its forty-two square, clumsy letters never won much popularity despite Kublai's proclamation that the Phags-pa script be used everywhere in the empire.

Phags-pa founded, with Kublai's blessing, many Lamaist monasteries. China alone had some 40,000, one of them with 213,000 monks and nuns. Phags-pa's native Tibet was almost entirely a religious state. Tibetan lamas occupied high positions in Kublai's government after the conquest of Sung China, and their greed and cruelty became legendary to the Chinese. One lama robbed the tombs of the Sung Dynasty.

Under Phags-pa's urgings, Kublai began to persecute the three main religious faiths of conquered China—Buddhism, Taoism, and Confucianism. Earlier he had supported all three, as other Mongol rulers had done, but now the Great Khan came to see the Chinese religions as threats to his own security. The native religious leaders, he felt, might become the instigators of rebellion. He preferred to root out these religions and replace them with Lamaism, which he could control through Phags-pa.

Taoism was the first religion to suffer. Originally a lofty

philosophy, it had become encrusted with superstition and mysticism, and Kublai disliked it. He ordered that all Taoist books be seized and burned. Only a few fragments of the extensive Taoist religious literature survived, and the faith itself became a troublesome underground movement.

Next Kublai let himself be persuaded to exclude all Confucianists from his court and from high government posts. For fifteen centuries the Chinese civil service had been made up almost entirely of Confucianists. Kublai found that it was impossible to remove them altogether, but he saw to it that they got the lowest positions in the administration, and filled the top ranks with Lamaists, Moslems, and Christians.

Even the Moslems came in for difficulties. For seven years their rituals were banned by Kublai, until he realized that the Moslem merchants and administrators in his realm were too valuable to him to merit this sort of treatment. Phags-pa also succeeded in downgrading the Chinese Buddhists, whom he particularly disliked because his own creed was a variation of theirs. The Buddhists were monks and peaceful scholars who had no interest in sorcery, and Kublai himself enjoyed their company. Despite Phags-pa's campaign against them, the Buddhists continued to have influence with the Great Khan. For most of his reign the two Buddhist sects—Chinese and Tibetan—vied with each other for Kublai's affection.

Marco Polo, who as a Christian lumped all these Asian faiths together as "idolatry," did not have much inkling of the rivalries between them. He knew that some religions were favored by the Great Khan and others were looked upon coolly. Still, even during this period when Kublai had departed from the traditional Mongol tolerance for all religions, it seemed to Marco as though the Khan was a model of religious liberalism. After all, Marco came from a Europe where only one religion—Catholic Christianity—was permitted. Moslems were regarded as deadly enemies and Jews were forbidden the rights of citizenship. Even Christians who dared to worship in a manner slightly different from the accepted way were tortured and put to painful death. Coming from this continent of bigotry, the young Venetian must have been dazzled by the presence of so many creeds at Kublai's court, the Lamaists predominant but the Buddhists, Moslems, Nestorians, and others all permitted to practice their worship and to preach to the Great Khan.

Kublai's main purpose in all this was to cement his grip on his empire. With just a few hundred thousand men he had to keep a population of close to a hundred million under control, a task that took all his considerable cleverness. A really determined Chinese leader who could gather popular support might succeed in overthrowing the Mongol rule, Kublai knew. For that reason, he kept strict watch on his subjects, giving the Chinese only subordinate positions.

When he took Chinese soldiers into his army, he was careful to station southern Chinese in Khitai and northern Chinese in what had been Sung China; he transferred his regiments frequently from place to place so the seeds of rebellion could not sprout. And he staffed his administration with capable foreigners loyal only to him.

Marco Polo became a member of that administration. Year after year he traveled through Kublai's empire on diplomatic missions. For three years he was governor of the huge city of Yangchow. He held other official positions too, although he does not name them for us. Wherever he went, Marco served as the Great Khan's eyes, noting down the curiosities of the vast and splendid realm. On his first journey, he went westward out of Cambaluc through the land he called Cathay (Khitai), past one wealthy city after another, jotting down his observations. Often his journal was repetitious; again and again he wrote: "The city is thriving with trade and handicrafts. They have great quantities of silk. Gold and silver cloths of all kinds are made there." The wealth of Cathay astounded him. So, too, did the upper Yangtze River:

"Along this river stand many cities and towns. There is great shipping on it, I mean an immense multitude of ships, such a number as no one who has not seen them could ever credit. The amount and quantity of great merchandise that traders carry up and down this river is also so vast, that no one who has not seen it could believe it. So big is the river that you would rather think it a sea than a river."

In Tibet Marco saw dogs "as big as donkeys." Without regret he left that cold, mountainous country and veered southeastward into Yunnan, the scene of Kublai's great military triumph a quarter of a century before. From Yunnan Marco sent the Great Khan a description of an unusual beast that must have fascinated the curiosity-loving Kublai:

"In this province there are great snakes or serpents of such immeasurable size as to strike you dumb; and they are truly hideous, both to look upon and to hear of. I will tell you how big and long they are. Know, then, that in very truth there are some ten paces long, as big as a large cask, for they have a girth of some ten palms. These are the biggest. In front, near the head, they have two short legs, without feet, but furnished with three claws, one large and two small, like those of falcons and lions. They have a very big head, and eyes larger than a big loaf; their mouth is so big that they can swallow a man whole; their teeth are enormous. They are so immeasurably large and fierce, that there is no man or beast that does not fear them."

It was perhaps the first time in history that a citizen of Venice had beheld a crocodile.

Marco's travels brought him to the northern frontiers of Burma before he returned to Cambaluc to pour out his wonders for the delighted Kublai Khan. On a later journey he entered Sung China, which he called *Manzi*. That name came from an old north Chinese nickname for the southerners: *man-tzu*, "southern ruffians." The cities of Cathay were as villages compared with the populous, enormously wealthy metropolises of Manzi. Marco wrote rapturously of these great walled cities, overflowing with silks and porcelains, though when he came to mighty Quinsay, the recently conquered Sung capital, words nearly failed him at its magnificence. He described it in careful detail, for Kublai had never visited this part of his empire.

No novelty escaped Marco. While in Cathay, he encountered a "kind of stone that burns like wood. These stones are dug out of the mountains like any other kind of stone, and make no flame, except a little at the beginning when they are lit, like charcoal, and by merely remaining red-hot they give out great heat." Coal—for so it was—was nothing new to Kublai, but apparently the Venetian had never heard of it before. Another wonder of Cathay was asbestos, a substance taken from mountains and crushed so that "it divides as it were into fibres of wool, which they set forth to dry. . . . These were then spun, and made into napkins. When first made these napkins are not very white, but by putting them into the fire for a while they come out as white as snow." Kublai had a wrapper of asbestos made as a gift for the Pope, and the Polos took it with them to Italy many years later when they left Cathay.

We may be sure that the Great Khan was well pleased

with young Marco. Of all the European visitors to Cathay in the thirteenth century, he alone had come neither to preach nor to engage in trade, but simply to see and learn. There were many foreigners at the court of Kublai Khan, and among them Marco Polo of Venice must have been the monarch's favorite.

SEVEN · *The Son of Heaven*

FROM 1279 Kublai was supreme in nearly all of Asia. His word was law over thousands of miles—a greater empire than any man had ruled before. Of course, in the West he did not have full control over his vassals of the Golden Horde and the Persian Il-khanate, but they respected his commands and obeyed them whenever possible. When Hulagu Khan died in 1264, his son Abaqa did not take the title of Il-khan until Kublai had sent his blessing. "Kublai is our ruler," he explained. "How dare I mount the throne without his approval?" The Golden Horde of Russia was more independent, but when Kublai requested soldiers from the Russian steppes to aid him in his Asiatic military campaigns, the successors of Batu and Bereke supplied them. Travelers passed in safety between Kublai's realm and the West, for the disciplined Mongols maintained order everywhere in their domain.

And in China Kublai was more than a Mongol khan. He was *Tien-tzu*, the Son of Heaven. The Chinese had long believed that their Emperor ruled by the decree of Heaven, and that all men were bound to obey. When a monarch lost the favor of Heaven, it was the right and even the duty of the new Son of Heaven to cast him down and rule in his place. This was known as "the changing of the Decree." Many dynasties had risen and fallen in China, and each time a new one came to power it was understood that Heaven had dictated a changing of the Decree. Some dynasties, like the T'ang and Sung, had lasted for hundreds of years. Others had slipped from sight in a few decades. Now it was the turn of the Yuan Dynasty of the Mongols to rule, and the Chinese sighed and told themselves that Heaven had withdrawn its favor from the Sung and bestowed it upon the Yuan, and that Kublai must be hailed as a legitimate Emperor of China, the true heir to the many dynasties of the past.

Kublai had always been drawn to Chinese civilization, and nothing pleased him more than to take on the role of Son of Heaven. He hoped that his accomplishments would match those of China's greatest rulers of the past. He admired Ch'in Shih Huang Ti, who had built the Great Wall of China in 221 B.C., but he hoped to match that Emperor's great achievement without resorting to his cruelty. He had high regard for Wu Ti of the Han Dynasty, who had come to power in 140 B.C. and was the first Chinese Emperor to open trade with the West. He respected the potent T'ai Tsung of the T'ang Dynasty, who had crushed China's enemies and built a great empire after taking the throne in A.D. 626. Kublai saw himself as the latest member of that heroic line.

He hoped to be an Emperor of peace and reform, not of tyranny and bloodshed. China was basically an agricultural country, and Kublai did battle against its three great foes, plague, famine, and drought. He distributed land and seed to the peasants and financed the construction of irrigation canals and flood-control dams. China's fields of rice and wheat were needed to support Kublai's huge military machine, and he wanted those fields to be productive. Before his time, Mongols knew nothing about agriculture, and scorned all peasants and farmers. In one of his most remarkable intellectual feats, Kublai rose above his nomad heritage to make himself an expert on the needs of a farming economy.

The Sung Emperors in the later years of their dynasty had left the peasants to withstand years of poor harvests unaided. Kublai wisely exercised greater control over the fluctuating yields of China's farms. From Marco Polo we learn that "when the Emperor sees that grain is cheap and abundant, he buys up large quantities, and has it stored in all his provinces in great granaries, where it is so well looked after that it will keep for three or four years. And this applies, let me tell you, to all kinds of grain, whether wheat, barley, millet, rice, or what not, and when there is any scarcity of a particular kind of grain, he causes that to be issued. And if the price of corn is at one gold piece the measure, he lets them have it at a gold piece for four measures, or at whatever price will produce general cheapness; and every one can have food in this way."

Even when the harvests failed through drought or flood, heat or cold, Kublai's bulging granaries kept the people from starvation. In districts where such calamities had struck, the Emperor decreed that taxes be omitted that year and provided grain for seed to bring forth next year's crop. In Cambaluc itself, Kublai ordered regular distributions of food to the poor. Anyone who wished could go to the royal bakeries each day and, so Marco says, "receive a great loaf apiece, hot from the baking, and nobody is denied. . . . And so some 30,000 people go for it every day from year's end to year's end." The weavers of fabrics had to pay a tax in services, working one day a week to make garments that Kublai distributed to poor families. Hospitals were founded to care for the sick.

All this was very far from the customs of the Mongols, who did not believe in charity. In Genghis Khan's day, when a beggar approached a Mongol he would be driven off harshly and told, "You bear God's curse, for if He loved you as He loves me, He would have provided for you!" Those Mongols who still followed the old ways were amazed to learn that their Great Khan was actually taking from the strong to aid the sick and elderly.

A good system of communications was essential in a country as huge as China. Roads were necessary so that food could be transported rapidly from the fields to the cities—and also so the Mongol horsemen could move swiftly to put down a rebellion in any part of the land. Marco Polo writes that Kublai ordered "all the highways traveled by his messengers and the people generally should be planted with rows of great trees a few paces apart; and thus these trees are visible a long way off, and no one can miss the way by day or night. Even the roads through uninhabited tracts are thus planted, and it is the greatest possible solace to travelers." According to Marco, Kublai took special pleasure in planting these trees, "because his astrologers and diviners tell him that he who plants trees lives long. But where the ground is so sandy and desert that trees will not grow, he causes other landmarks, pillars or stones, to be set up to show the way."

The Emperor's advisers pointed out the value of good water transportation to link the various parts of China, and he agreed. In early China, problems had arisen because the chief food-producing regions were in the south, while the main zone of military action was in the north, along the Great Wall frontier. That had been solved in A.D. 610 by the construction of the Grand Canal, which connected the rich rice lands of the Yangtze delta with the two inland capital cities of the north. In the following six and a half centuries the canal had been allowed to fall into disrepair. Moreover, the political center of China had shifted eastward to the new capital at Cambaluc. So Kublai dictated the construction of a second Grand Canal, an inland waterway that would carry tons of rice to the north.

It was a monumental project that took some twenty years to complete and employed millions of laborers. Not until 1289, when Kublai was seventy-five years old, was the new Grand Canal completed. By then a splendid paved highway ran beside its banks, eleven hundred miles long, linking Quinsay to Cambaluc—that is, from Hangchow to Peking. At places along this canal the Chinese engineers built systems of locks to permit great vessels to pass through shallow water. Rashid-ad-Din, the Persian historian who wrote at the end of the thirteenth century, informs us that "the canal is provided with many sluices . . . and when vessels arrive at these sluices they are hoisted up by means of machinery, whatever be their size, and let down on the other side into the water. . . . Along the side of the canal runs the high road, extending for a space of forty days' journey, and this has been paved throughout, so that travelers and their animals may get along during the rainy season without sinking in the mud. . . . Shops, taverns, and villages line the road on both sides, so that dwelling succeeds dwelling without intermission throughout the whole space of forty days' journey."

At the capital, the Emperor collected painters, scholars, poets, architects, and engineers from far parts of the world. He had an astronomical observatory built at Cambaluc and ordered careful records kept of the movements of the stars. The calendar was revised to make it more accurate. History, mathematics, and geography were encouraged. Kublai commanded that dictionaries of the various languages of China be compiled, and the job was done so well that some of them are still in use today. Many books came from the printing presses of China, including works in two forms previously unfamiliar in that country, the novel and the play.

It was a prosperous time, a busy time. Rarely had China had such a gifted, enlightened Emperor. There was work for all, and few went hungry. The historians had to look back more than five centuries, to the finest moments of the T'ang Dynasty, for a comparable era of fruitfulness in China.

Yet the fact remained that the Mongols were ruling China as conquerors, and they were hated for that reason. Perhaps the Chinese thought warmly of Kublai Khan himself, but they loathed his foreign-born ministers. The Mongols had had no experience in governing a country like China, and Kublai's wise decrees were not always carried out properly. The landlords and the governors flourished, but the peasants often were oppressed. Marco Polo, who rarely could bring himself to write anything uncomplimentary to his master, found it necessary to remark that in every province "there were many disloyal and seditious persons, at all times disposed to break out in rebellion," and therefore Mongol garrisons had to be stationed outside all large cities to keep the peace.

In the early years of Kublai's reign, the people were so happy to know peace again that they rarely expressed any hostility toward their conquerors. Kublai's wisdom and charity won him many supporters. However, the Chinese slowly grew disenchanted with the Great Khan. His fondness for luxury led him to build ever more extravagant palaces—using Chinese labor and Chinese wealth. The taxes paid by the Chinese went to pay the Mongol and Turkish soldiers Kublai used in his many military adventures. Kublai's palaces and Kublai's armies became a severe drain on the Chinese economy, and created great hardships. Famines occurred despite the system of public granaries, and the population declined. There had been a hundred million Chinese in 1125; two hundred years later, after half a century of Mongol rule, the census showed a population of only forty-five million, and seven and a half million of those were officially listed as "starving."

One difficulty was Kublai's habit of taking the advice of men he should not have heeded—perhaps his greatest weakness. On religious matters, he gave too much authority to the sinister lama Phags-pa. In the field of economics, Kublai let himself be swayed by a Persian financial expert named Ahmad, who was given great power by the Em-

peror in 1270. It was Ahmad's job to raise the money that
Kublai needed for his great expenditures. During his
twelve years of rule, Ahmad milked the country dry, ex-
torting cruel taxes that not only covered Kublai's expenses
but went to line his own pockets.

Ahmad's method of getting money involved the use of
paper money. At that time, most of the world used only
precious metal—gold or silver—as currency. In China,
the T'ang Dynasty had permitted private bankers to issue
paper money backed by an equivalent amount of copper
coins. Under the Sung Dynasty that followed, the government issued its own paper money, also backed by copper.
As the Sung power weakened, its paper money gradually
became worthless when the backing was withdrawn.

Kublai found the concept of paper money appealing.
In 1260, the first year of his reign as Great Khan, he issued
such currency to meet the huge expenses of his wars against
Sung China and his own Mongol rivals. When China fell,
Kublai extended the use of his paper money to the con-
quered territory. His expenses kept growing.

The scheming Ahmad persuaded Kublai to issue more
and more and more paper money. It was simplicity itself,
Ahmad said: the government would collect its taxes in
goods of real value, like wheat, rice, furs, and silk. When
it had to meet its expenses, it would pay its bills with paper.
By government decree the paper currency would be worth
the face value printed on it—and who could dare to defy

an imperial decree? So long as the word of the Emperor was law, he could go on manufacturing as much paper money as he needed.

Marco Polo thought the system was delightful. He wrote: "The Emperor makes his money after this fashion. From the bark of a tree, the mulberry tree, the leaves of which feed the silkworms, the fine inner skin is taken. This is made into something like sheets of paper. These sheets, which are black, are cut up into different sizes. . . . All these pieces of paper are printed with as much care as if they were actually pure gold or silver. On every piece officials write their names; then the chief officer of the Khan puts red vermilion on the state seal and stamps it upon the paper. The money is then authorized. And anyone forging it may be put to death.

"And the Khan causes such a vast amount of this paper money—which costs him nothing—to be made each year that it must equal all the other treasures of the world.

"These pieces of paper he makes pass wherever his sovereignty extends, in all territories, and with them he makes all payments on his own account. Nobody, however great in rank, dares refuse them. And, indeed, the people take them readily because with them sales and purchases of goods can be transacted as well as with coins of gold or silver.

"More than that, merchants arriving from India or foreign lands, bringing with them gold, silver, precious stones, and pearls, are forbidden to sell to anyone but the Emperor's treasurer. He has twelve expert appraisers to buy in this way, at liberal prices, with these pieces of paper. . . . So the Khan buys up such a quantity that his treasure grows beyond count, while the paper money he pays out costs him nothing!"

Anyone who wished could redeem his paper money by turning it in at the imperial mint for gold and silver. To discourage such redemptions, though, Ahmad decreed that one could get in precious metals only *half* the value printed on the face of each note. Since few were willing to do this, the paper money had to circulate in the absence of any stronger currency.

Marco Polo was no expert on economics, and, alas, neither was Kublai Khan. It should have been easy to predict what would happen. The country was flooded with paper money as Kublai's expenditures multiplied. In 1269, the paper money in circulation had a face value in silver of 228,960 ounces. By 1290, the figure had risen to 50,002,-500 ounces.

The Emperor could compel the people to accept his paper money, but he could not force them to maintain its value. The more there was in circulation, the less each note would buy—a process familiar to us as inflation. A merchant who had charged two pieces of silver for goods in 1270 (taking paper money for his payment) might ask ten or fifteen pieces of silver (again, accepting paper) for the same goods a dozen years later.

The value of the paper notes dropped steeply. In 1287,

the Mongol treasury had to call in all the old paper money and issue new notes, at a rate of one new note for each five old ones. The new money still sank in purchasing power, so that in 1309 another one-for-five exchange was ordered. That meant that the value of Mongol currency fell twenty-fivefold in half a century. In our terms, it would mean that a quarter would come to buy no more than a single cent does today; it would cost more than a dollar to mail a letter, five dollars to buy a frankfurter, forty dollars to go to the movies.

Kublai Khan was not alive to see the final catastrophic collapse of his paper money, though much of its decline occurred in his lifetime. Nor was the minister Ahmad on the scene. The Chinese rightly identified him as the cause of their economic woes and eventually removed him. They did not blame Kublai. "He loved his people," a Chinese chronicler wrote, "and he had only one grievous failing— he placed foreigners in supreme authority over the people."

The Chinese hated Ahmad, for he wrung them dry and stocked his own house with stolen treasures. He made the Chinese give him heavy bribes, and forced their most beautiful women to join his harem. Anyone who displeased Ahmad was put to death. Kublai, who was growing old and no longer paid as much attention to the government as he once had, was blind to Ahmad's misdeeds.

In 1282, while Kublai was away from the capital on a hunting expedition, the Chinese launched a revolt to overthrow Ahmad. The ringleaders were Cheng-y, a government official who had suffered greatly at Ahmad's hands, and Wang Chu, a Chinese officer in the Mongol army.

After dark one evening the conspirators entered the royal palace and sent a message to Ahmad, saying that Chingkim, Kublai's eldest son, had arrived in the capital unexpectedly and wished to see the finance minister at once. Ahmad hurried to the palace.

As he reached the gate, he met a Mongol named Kogatai, the commander of the capital's defending garrison. "Where are you bound so late?" Kogatai asked him.

"To see Chingkim, who has just arrived," Ahmad answered.

"How can that be? How could he arrive so secretly that I know nothing of it?"

Ahmad did not know. Suspicious, Kogatai and some of his soldiers accompanied Ahmad into the palace.

The conspirators had lit bright lights in the great hall. Ahmad entered. Unable to see clearly in the glare, he knelt before Wang Chu, thinking him to be Chingkim. Cheng-y, who was hidden nearby, stepped forward and cut off the finance minister's head.

It could have been the start of a general uprising that would drive the Mongols out of the capital. But Kogatai burst into the hall, crying, "Treason!" He shot an arrow at Wang Chu, killing him. Cheng-y was taken prisoner, and the conspiracy subsided once its leaders were removed. In the morning, Kogatai rounded up all who had had any part in the plot and put them to death.

Messengers brought the word to Kublai, and he hurried back to Cambaluc to find out what had taken place. Those who had never dared to speak to the Emperor about the wickedness of Ahmad, for fear of the minister's vengeance, now came forward. Marco informs us that Kublai "learned all about the endless iniquities of that accursed Ahmad and his sons. . . . The Great Khan then ordered all the treasure that Ahmad had accumulated in the Old City to be transferred to his own treasury in the New City, and it was found to be of enormous amount. He also ordered the body of Ahmad to be dug up and cast into the streets for the dogs to tear; and he commanded those of Ahmad's sons who had followed the father's evil example to be flayed alive."

Thus did the Son of Heaven belatedly punish the injustices committed by Ahmad. It was too late, though, to undo the damage that the minister had caused in the twelve years that he guided Kublai Khan's financial policies.

When oppressed by such cares of office, Kublai found relaxation in one of his many palaces. In the magnificent city of Cambaluc the Emperor could never escape from the routines of duty, but north of the Great Wall he had his beloved country retreat of Shang-tu, with its parks and its lakes, and as the years passed he added other royal lodgings elsewhere in Mongolia. One of his favorites was the palace at Chagan-nor ("White Lake"), which was constructed in 1280. "He likes much to reside there," Marco Polo declares, "on account of the lakes and rivers in the neighborhood, which are the haunt of swans and of a great variety of other birds. The adjoining plains too abound with cranes, partridges, pheasants, and other game birds, so that the Emperor takes all the more delight in staying there, in order to go a-hawking with his falcons, a sport of which he is very fond."

Kublai Khan divided his year according to a formal pattern of annual migrations—the last remnant, perhaps, of his nomad ancestry. From September to February he remained at Cambaluc, overseeing the details of government. Then he embarked on a three-month hunting expedition through the wooded areas of the northeast. This took him in a great circle back to Cambaluc by the middle of May; he remained there only three days this time, holding court and staging a splendid feast. The next stop was Chagan-nor, where the Great Khan spent a few weeks hunting and fowling on the lakes, and by June he arrived at Shang-tu to pass the summer. Late in August, it was time to move again: back to Chagan-nor for several days of amusement, and on to Cambaluc for the six-month winter season of administrative chores.

The months at Cambaluc were punctuated with colorful festivals held in the great hall of Kublai's palace. The Emperor's table, at the north end of this enormous chamber, was elevated above all others, so that he could look down on his thousands of guests. His chief wife, the lady Jamui, sat beside him on his left. On his right sat his sons and nephews, and other princes of the royal blood, their tables placed so that their heads were no higher than the Emperor's feet. The others, both Mongol and Chinese, sat at a still lower level, many of them on carpets rather than chairs.

Marco Polo informs us that "in a certain part of the hall near where the Great Khan holds his table, there is a buffet about three paces on each side, beautifully wrought with figures of animals, carved and gilded. In it stands a great vessel of pure gold from which wine flavored with fine and costly spices is drawn off." Golden pitchers, big enough to hold drink for eight or ten persons, were set on the tables so that each feaster could help himself to the spiced wine.

Mongol nobles served Kublai his food, their faces covered with fine napkins of silk and gold so their breath might not taint the flavor of the Emperor's repast. Each time Kublai put his wine goblet to his lips, Marco says, the entire assemblage fell to its knees and bowed low to him. Since Kublai grew increasingly fond of his wine as he gained in years, the guests at his feasts must have been on their knees most of the time; but of this Marco says nothing.

When the tables were cleared, jugglers and acrobats came prancing into the hall, and magicians demonstrated their sorcery. The entertainment, we read, "creates great diversion and mirth, so that everybody is full of laughter and enjoyment. And when the performance is over, the company breaks up and everyone goes to his quarters."

The most spectacular festival of the year was Kublai's birthday party, held on the twenty-eighth of September. Marco Polo's account indicates some of the splendor of this glittering event:

"On his birthday, the Great Khan dresses in the best of his robes, all wrought with beaten gold; and twelve thousand barons and knights on that day come forth dressed in robes of the same color, and precisely like those of the Great Khan, except that they are not so costly; but still they are all of the same color as his, and are also of silk and gold. Every one of them has a great golden belt. This raiment is given them by the Great Khan. And I assure you that some of these robes are decked with so many pearls and precious stones that a single suit is worth ten thousand pieces of gold.

"And of such raiment there are several sets. For you must know that the Great Khan, thirteen times in the year, presents to his barons and knights such suits as I am speaking of. And on each occasion they wear the same color as he does, a different color being assigned to each festival. It is truly a wondrous thing, as you may see, and no prince in the world but he could possibly keep up such customs as these.

"On his birthday, all the Tartars in the world, and all the countries and governments that owe allegiance to the Khan, offer him great presents. . . . And on this day likewise all the Idolaters, all the Saracens [Moslems], and all the Christians and other descriptions of people make great and solemn devotions, with much chanting and lighting of lamps and burning of incense, each to the god that he doth worship, praying that he would save the Emperor, and grant him long life and health and happiness."

Nearly as impressive was the festival of the New Year, held in February. The Khan and all his subjects clad themselves in robes of white, a color the Mongols believed was lucky. (The Chinese, who have always regarded white as a color of mourning, prohibited the wearing of white clothes on New Year's Day when they ruled their own land.) Once again ambassadors came to the Emperor, bringing "presents of gold and silver, and pearls and gems, and rich textures of divers kinds." Each province sent a gift, and where possible sent eighty-one gifts, or nine times nine, since nine was deemed a lucky number by the Mongols. Marco claims that "on that day more than 100,000 white horses are presented to the Khan," probably something of an exaggeration. He also writes that "on that day the whole of the Khan's elephants, fully 5000 in number, are exhibited, all covered with rich and gay housings of inlaid cloth representing beasts and birds, while each of them carries on his back two splendid coffers filled with golden dishes to be used at the feast." When the tables were set, the entire company filed into the great hall, taking seats in order of rank. A court official would cry in a booming voice, "Bow and adore!" It was the signal to all to drop to their knees and touch their foreheads to the ground in honor of Kublai Khan. The feast would follow; and then the jugglers and clowns arrived to end the festivities.

The same pomp and grandeur marked Kublai's hunting expeditions. In his younger days, he had done his hunting in the Mongol fashion, from the back of a fast-moving steed. But the Great Khan was sixty-five years old when he became Son of Heaven, and no longer fit for such strenuous amusements. His physical strength and endurance was as great as ever, but he had grown bulky in a long and well-fed life, and his gout prevented him from riding.

Abandoning his Mongolian thoroughbreds, the Great Khan rode to the hunt in a wooden pavilion, lined within with plates of gold and bedecked outside with tiger skins, carried on the back of an elephant. Sheltered in this comfortable closed chamber, Kublai took his ease while the great beast lumbered along. He kept several of his choicest hunting falcons in the pavilion with him, and was attended by the nobles of his court, who rode on horseback beside the Khan and carried on conversation with him.

When the prey was sighted—a crane, perhaps, or a partridge—one of these courtiers would cry out to the Emperor, who instantly had the roof of his pavilion drawn back to loose one of his falcons. "And often the quarry is struck within his view," Marco relates, "so that he has the most exquisite sport and diversion, there as he sits in his chamber or lies on his bed; and all the barons with him get the enjoyment of it likewise! So it is not without reason I tell you that I do not believe there ever existed in the world or ever will exist, a man with such sport and enjoyment as he has, or with such rare opportunities."

When the hunting expedition of Kublai Khan took to the fields each March, it was like an army going to the wars. Ten thousand servants attended him. They cared for the fierce hunting birds: Kublai's five hundred falcons and his many varieties of hawks. These thousands of men fanned out in groups of one or two hundred just ahead of the Khan's party, each group carrying a hunting bird. The hawks and falcons bore labels on their legs, with the names of their keepers, so that when a bird had gone aloft to pounce on its prey and descended with it, bird and catch could be taken to the proper attendant. Whenever the Emperor himself let loose a falcon, one of these men followed it in its flight until it came down.

The Khan's favorite hunting place was known as Cachar Modun, northeast of the Great Wall. Here a great camp was pitched each year, with thousands of tents, for the entire Mongol aristocracy accompanied Kublai on these expeditions. There they remained from the middle of

March to the middle of May. "And all that time," Marco declares, "he does nothing but go hawking round about among the cane brakes along the lakes and rivers that abound in that region, and across fine plains on which are plenty of cranes and swans, and all sorts of other fowl. The other gentry of the camp also are never done with hunting and hawking, and every day they bring home great store of venison and feathered game of all sorts."

To insure a dependable supply of game for the Khan's amusement, no subject who lived within twenty days' journey from Cachar Modun was permitted to own hawks or hounds, and everywhere in the empire the hunting of hares, stags, bucks, and roes was prohibited between March and October. "Anybody who should do so would rue it bitterly," says Marco Polo. "But those people are so obedient to their lord's command, that even if a man were to find one of those animals asleep by a roadside he would not touch it for the world! And thus the game multiplies at such a rate that the whole country swarms with it, and the Emperor gets as much as he could desire. Aside from the span from March to October, every subject may hunt these animals as he wishes."

Kublai's hunting sometimes served a useful purpose for the common people. One season there were so many rabbits in a certain province that the crops were being destroyed. The people of that province made application to the Emperor, who came there with all his court to hunt.

When he left, the rabbit population in that district no longer was a problem.

Another of Kublai's passions was the collecting of rare and beautiful things. His palaces gleamed with such wonders as a ruby from Siam the size of a man's fist, dark vessels of jade from Khotan, matched pearls as big as birds' eggs, carved elephant tusks. When word reached him of a certain bird called the Rukh, found on the isle of Madagascar, so huge that it could snatch an elephant with its talons and carry it to its nest, Kublai sent an ambassador across the Indian Ocean to obtain its feathers. And, so Marco Polo solemnly asserts, Kublai received a single feather of this bird that was ninety hand-spans long, with a quill two palms-widths around. (One botanist has suggested that what arrived at Cambaluc was actually the frond of the Raphia palm, which can be thirty-five to forty feet long and a foot thick at the stem, and in dried form resembles the feather of a monstrous bird.)

Kublai also collected fair women. Jamui, the bride of his youth, remained at his side until her death in 1281, and was always his favorite among women. However, the Khan had three other wives, and each had a court of her own, with three hundred handmaidens apiece to serve her, and hundreds of pages and slaves. Besides these, the Khan maintained a harem of dozens of beautiful Chinese and Mongol girls. Each year, the hundred fairest girls in the realm were sent to the court of Kublai, where certain sharp-eyed old women selected the ones best suited to join Kublai's harem. According to Marco Polo, Kublai had twenty-two sons by his four official wives, and twenty-five more by his concubines. Seven of his sons were made governors of outlying provinces, while the eldest, Chingkim, remained close by Kublai's side so that he could learn the task of ruling the empire.

The Son of Heaven lived well. Age rested lightly on him, fat and gouty though he grew. His life was a constant round of pleasure, and he loved flamboyant displays of grandeur and pomp in an almost childlike way. The Mongol side of his nature showed in this fondness for great gaudy festivals; but at the same time he could be shrewd and crafty, a capable ruler, a strange mixture of barbarism and sophistication. Asia had never seen anyone quite like him before. He fascinated everyone, particularly Marco Polo.

"Kublai is of a good stature," Marco wrote, "neither tall nor short, but of middle height. He has a becoming amount of flesh, and is very shapely in all his limbs. His complexion is white and red, the eyes black and fine, the nose well formed and well set on. . . . He is, I tell you, the wisest and most accomplished man, the greatest captain, the best to govern men and rule an empire, as well as the most valiant, that ever has existed among all the tribes of Tartars."

EIGHT · *Military Adventures*

THOUGH HE lived in unimaginable splendor, Kublai Khan could never forget that he was a Mongol and the grandson of Genghis Khan. The Mongol heritage was upon him: to conquer the world, to carry the *yasas* to the corners of the globe.

Kublai was too realistic to think that he could be a true world-conqueror. Europe lay beyond his reach. In the days of Batu, when the Mongol empire had been young and bursting with energy, Europe would have fallen to the nomad hordes but for the timely death of the Great Khan Ogodai. Now, after decades of civil war, the old outward spirit was gone. The Golden Horde, the western branch of the Mongols, held Russia in an iron grip, but showed little interest in a new invasion of Western Europe, and Kublai did not care to prod Batu's descendants into making the attempt. Similarly, the Il-khans had settled comfortably in Persia and had all but given up Hulagu's old ambition to conquer Egypt and Syria.

Asia, though, was Kublai's realm—and in Asia he carried out the commandment of Genghis, almost from force of habit, sending armies of conquest to neighboring lands merely because they were there and tempted him to subjugate them. All through his long reign as Great Khan, Kublai launched these military adventures as if stubbornly determined to show that there was Mongol blood in his veins. The results, however, were hardly impressive.

His first campaign after proclaiming himself Great Khan in 1260 was directed against fellow Mongols, not foreign lands. It was his war against the followers of his brother Arik-buga, which met with quick success. Arik-buga's army was easily defeated, though he managed to continue an ineffectual guerrilla attack until 1264.

By 1268, Kublai was ready to finish the conquest of China. As we have seen, it took eleven years to carry this out, though from 1276 on the Sung resistance was confined to southeastern China alone. This war was Kublai's greatest military success; he himself never took part in the actual combat, however.

In the same year that he sent Bayan against the Sung, Kublai found himself at war with his nephew Kaidu. Kaidu, the grandson of Ogodai, was the leader of the tradition-keeping nomad Mongols of Central Asia. Proud, fearless, fiery, Kaidu was closest of all of the Mongols of his time to the spirit of Genghis Khan. Like Genghis, he began with a handful of supporters and built an army by sheer force of personality.

When still a very young man, Kaidu had fought heroically in the Mongol invasion of Europe. During the brief reign of his uncle, the Great Khan Kuyuk, Kaidu had been a figure of some importance at Karakorum. When Mangu came to power in 1251, he found it necessary to wipe out most of the house of Ogodai, and though Kaidu was spared he bore hatred ever after toward the sons of Tului.

Kaidu hotly refused to pay homage when Kublai Khan took the throne. Kublai invited his nephew to visit him and pledge allegiance, and Kaidu returned the mocking reply, "My horses are sick." He fled with a few men into the rugged steppes of Central Asia after the defeat of Arikbuga. Collecting an ever-growing force of disgruntled Mongols who had no love for the extravagant, over-civilized Kublai, Kaidu ranged through the forests and mountains west of China, raiding at will.

He made war against Kublai in the old nomad manner: striking swiftly, retreating into the deserts of the north before a counterattack was possible. Nimble parties of Kaidu's marauders struck like lightning along Kublai's northern frontier. The Great Khan found himself in the position of all Chinese Emperors under nomad attack: unable to do much about it. It had never been practical to send an army into the north to deal with such raiders, for the nomads would simply scatter in all directions. The Chinese had tried to defend themselves by building the Great Wall, but even that had only limited value. Kublai dealt with Kaidu by stationing garrisons in the north, a screen of cavalry units flanking the borders of Kaidu's territory. When Kaidu's strength reached a peak, he attempted to break through the screen, and generally was driven back with heavy losses; but the Great Khan's troops could not pursue and destroy the enemy when Kaidu retreated deep into Mongolia. A permanent stalemate developed, long periods of uneasy waiting broken by occasional border skirmishes. Kublai found it irritating, since he was occupied with the war in China and did not wish to divert his able Mongol soldiers to the struggle with Kaidu. Year after year, decade after decade, Kaidu kept nibbling infuriatingly at Kublai's realm, cutting the lines of communication between the Great Khan and his vassals in Persia and Russia.

When it became apparent that Sung China was about to fall, Kublai committed his armies to yet another great enterprise: the conquest of Japan. As early as 1266, the Great Khan had hoped to master this group of islands northeast of his empire. Korean merchants visiting Kublai told him that the palaces of Japan were bright with golden ornaments, and that great rosy-hued pearls came from the sea off one of the Japanese islands.

Kublai had already brought Korea, Japan's neighbor, under his control—not by conquest but simply through an ultimatum. The Mongols had invaded Korea several times between 1231 and 1238; when Kublai came to the throne in 1260, he ordered the weak, unhappy Korean kingdom to accept Mongol rule, and the Koreans yielded. They became Mongol subjects, and though they had little liking for their new masters they took care not to offend them. Since the Mongols were not a seafaring people, Kublai intended to employ the nautical skills of the Koreans in his campaign against Japan.

He tried conquest-by-ultimatum on the Japanese first. In 1266 the Great Khan sent two envoys to Korea, where they were to take ship for Japan. They carried a message to the Japanese: "The Mongol power will be kind to you. It wishes that you become part of the great Mongol empire." The Koreans provided a vessel for the envoys, who set out for the nearest Japanese island, only a hundred miles from Korea's southern tip. When rough weather came up, the Korean sailors headed for their home port, apologetically telling the Mongol envoys that it was impossible to make the voyage. Meanwhile, Koreans who disliked Mongol rule sent word to Japan of Kublai's plans.

Angered that his message had not been delivered, Kublai sent more envoys at the beginning of 1268 with the same ultimatum. This time the message was received. Japan at that time had an extremely complex governmental system;

the Mikado, or Emperor, had become a powerless figure-head, and real power was in the hands of a family of heredi-tary dictators, the Hojos. The Mikado was terrified by Kublai's threat, but the dictator, Hojo Tokimune, re-mained calm. The Mongols, he said, were no sailors, and Japan could be invaded only by sea. Moreover, the highly trained Japanese warrior class would be a match for Kublai's barbaric soldiers, whose strike-and-run tactics of horsemanship would do them no good in a naval war. Tokimune chose to ignore the ultimatum, and haughtily sent the Mongol envoys home without a reply. Quietly he strengthened the shore defenses and ordered all mem-bers of the nobility to prepare their troops for war. Though he was only eighteen, Tokimune intended to defy the might of the Mongols.

The Koreans, who would be caught in the middle in a war between the Mongols and the Japanese, tried in vain to negotiate a settlement. In September 1271, Kublai sent a third message to Japan. This too was ignored, and still no Mongol invasion came. Kublai had actually been bluff-ing, for he was too busy with the war in China to make good his threats. Still hoping to frighten Japan into sur-rendering, late in 1272 the Great Khan sent another ambas-sador, who insisted on receiving a reply. The Japanese ex-pelled him. It amounted to a declaration of war.

The fall of the twin Han River fortresses in 1273 fore-shadowed the collapse of Sung China, and allowed Kublai to mount an expedition against Japan. He ordered the King of Korea to build warships for him and collect a large army. The Koreans, a poor and weak people, were slow to respond. Not until November 1274 was the navy ready: three hundred large vessels, four or five hundred small ones. Some seven thousand Korean and Chinese sailors manned these vessels. The invading army itself consisted of fifteen thousand crack Mongol and Chinese troops, and eight thousand badly trained Koreans.

The invaders landed on two small outlying Japanese islands and took them after fierce fighting. The fleet next turned southeast toward the large island of Kyushu, where landings were made at several points. The Japanese warriors gathered and marched toward the battle zone, bridging a river with pontoons so troops could be transported across it.

The Mongols seized a number of towns along the shore. On November 20, the defending Japanese army arrived, rapidly to discover that the Mongols were fiercer adversaries than had been anticipated. The veteran soldiers of Kublai Khan were trained to fight in close formation, while the aristocratic Japanese warriors were more accustomed to single combat. Kublai's men had been toughened by war against China, while the Japanese had seen no military action since a civil war more that fifty years earlier. Armed with powerful crossbows and the catapults that had proved successful against the Chinese, the soldiers of the Great Khan forced their way inland at heavy loss of Japanese life.

While waiting for reinforcements to come from other islands, the defenders dug in behind an ancient earthen wall a few miles from the shore. Their task was to hold out until aid came; Hojo Tokimune's strategy was based on the much greater numbers of the Japanese, who would eventually wear down the Mongols. That night thunder sounded in the distance, and the weatherwise Korean sailors sensed the approach of a great storm. That meant danger; a sudden typhoon might wreck the invading fleet and leave the Mongols with no line of retreat. It was a problem the Mongols had not considered. They were reluctant to give up their hard-won position simply because of the weather.

The storm broke. The Japanese might take advantage of the darkness, wind, and rain to leave their trenches and carry out a surprise attack over ground they knew well, the Mongols realized. Unwillingly they sounded the signal for a withdrawal, not knowing that the Japanese were too exhausted to fight. As the gale raged, the invaders boarded their ships and made for the open sea. Several vessels ran aground on a sandbar, and dozens more foundered in the storm. Korean records say that thirteen thousand of the Mongols were drowned during the retreat. When dawn broke, the surprised Japanese found the harbor clear of Mongol ships and the bodies of their foes littering the shore.

The shattered fleet straggled back to Korea in humiliation, and the Japanese rejoiced. Kublai, enraged by the defeat, let himself be persuaded that he would have conquered Japan but for the storm. He did not see that while the Mongols could take a few seacoast towns, they could not hope to crush all of Japan. It was impossible to land enough men to equal the strength of the Japanese army.

Still nourishing his dream of conquest, Kublai sent a new ultimatum to the Japanese Emperor, ordering him to present himself at Cambaluc to pay homage. Realizing that a second armada would soon be on its way, Hojo Tokimune mobilized his country and ordered a stone wall to be built along the coast of Kyushu where the Mongols had landed in 1274. When Kublai's envoys arrived in the spring of 1275, Tokimune had them put to death.

It was an insult Kublai could not fail to avenge. However, he had committed a huge force to the final conquest of Sung China, and Japan received a breathing spell. The unexpectedly stubborn Sung resistance along the southeastern coast entangled the Mongols in a naval war that did not end until 1279. With China at last under his control, Kublai ordered the King of Korea to build another fleet for the invasion of Japan.

This time Kublai planned to crush his foes beneath an

immense attack. He set up a special "Office for the Chastisement of Japan" to supervise the invasion. The shipyards of Korea worked day and night to construct ships. In addition, Kublai now had at his command the large navy of Sung China. Korea supplied nine hundred ships, fifteen thousand seamen, ten thousand fighting men. Kublai added to this force some thirty thousand of his own reliable Mongol and northern Chinese soldiers. In the south, a colossal fleet of Sung ships, bearing more than a hundred thousand southern Chinese troops, was readied. The combined armada was the largest single overseas expedition in history, and remained unmatched until the twentieth century.

The Korean-based fleet was ready to sail in the spring of 1281; the unwieldy southern Chinese fleet was delayed by provisioning problems. Without waiting for the larger force, the Korean-Mongol force struck at Japan in June. Once again small outlying islands fell first; then came the landing at Kyushu. A stone wall confronted the invaders. The Japanese defended the wall ably, and when the Mongols tried to go around its ends they were thrown back. For seven weeks the main line of defense was held. The Mongols found themselves pinned down to a narrow beachhead at Hakata Bay. The arrival of the Chinese ships did little to change the picture; the Chinese had no reason to exert themselves on behalf of their Mongol masters, and they fought half-heartedly at best. The presence of these hundred thousand men only added to the problems of the invaders, whose provisions were running low.

The Japanese held firm. They sent small craft stealing into Hakata Bay to harass the anchored Mongol fleet. For once the Mongols had met adversaries as valiant and as dogged as themselves.

The month of August is typhoon season in Japan. As had happened in 1274, a storm descended on the battle-field. Once again the Korean captains beat a hasty retreat, though not so hasty that they did not lose thousands of men; a third of the Korean and Mongol troops drowned in the storm as the ships tried to reach open water. The Chinese ships suffered even more severely. Caught in the full brunt of the storm, they went to the bottom by the hundreds, while the Japanese swarmed over their wall to slaughter the thousands of panicky men on the beach. The armada was wrecked. Great gusts of wind blew for two days, scattering the vessels like straws. The Japanese called the storm a *kamikaze*, "divine wind."

Those Mongols who did not drown were trapped on shore and put to death. The Chinese and Korean prisoners were taken into slavery. Scarcely a man escaped to bring the sorrowful tale to Kublai Khan.

The Japanese praised the *kamikaze* that had rescued them a second time in seven years. Kublai Khan, chagrined and dismayed, cursed the ill luck that sent storms to wreck his fleets. Against the advice of his ministers, he gave orders for a third armada to be constructed.

The Koreans, his shipbuilders, were exhausted by the war effort. They had ruined their economy to provide navies for Kublai Khan, and now they made it clear that they had no resources left. Kublai's Chinese sailors deserted and turned pirate, raiding the coasts of their own land rather than fight Japan again. By 1286, Kublai came to the humiliating realization that he could not send another invasion force against Japan. Other wars were in progress, and it was impossible to pursue the vain dream of Japanese conquest.

Until the Mongol landing of 1274, Japan had never been invaded by another power. The second Mongol invasion of 1281 proved to be the last Japan would know until our own time, and even then no successful naval landing on the Japanese islands was carried out in World War II before Japan surrendered. The dive-bombing "suicide planes" used by the Japanese in that war were known as *kamikaze,* in memory of the "divine wind" that had driven off the Mongols six hundred fifty years before.

Another of Kublai's military objectives was Southeast Asia: the peninsula that today is divided among the nations of Burma, Thailand, Malaysia, Cambodia, Laos, and Vietnam. This tropical, heavily forested region, inhabited by people of non-Chinese stock, has been a target of Chinese aggression for at least twenty-two hundred years. Ch'in Shih Huang Ti, China's first Emperor, invaded it about 213 B.C., getting as far as what is now North Vietnam. Later Chinese Emperors sent other expeditions there, invariably without success. And today's headlines testify that China still is attempting to bring the peninsula under her control.

The Great Khan himself had seen action in a nearby zone during his dramatic conquest of Yunnan in 1253–1254. He longed to add the kingdoms south of Yunnan to his realm. Remembering his own successful campaigns there, he refused to believe that his generals could fail to be victorious.

In 1277, when most of Sung China was in Kublai's hands, he sent an army to the border between Yunnan and Burma. The Mongols hacked their way through the dense jungles, slowed by the intense, smothering heat, the torrential rains, and the toll of tropical disease.

The King of Burma had expected an invasion from the north for many years, and his frontier was guarded. A well-trained army equipped with war elephants waited for the Mongols in the Burmese jungles. Marco Polo, whose travels on Kublai's behalf had taken him to Burma, told how the Mongol horses "took fright at the sight of the elephants and could not be got to face the foe, but always swerved and turned back; whilst all the time the king and his forces, and all his elephants, continued to advance upon them."

More than twenty years before, a Mongol army commanded by Uriangkatai had been in the same position and had thrown the charging elephants into disarray by shooting flaming arrows at them. It worked once again: "The elephants turned tail and fled toward the king's men, with such a noise and uproar that you would have thought the world was collapsing! When the Tartars saw that the enemy had turned tail, they hewed them down, and gave chase, slaying them so mercilessly that truly it was a pitiful sight to see."

The heavy cavalry of the Burmese failed, but other tactics kept the Mongols at bay. The jungle folk lurked in their forests, picking off the invaders with poisoned arrows. Heat and disease did the rest. The sweltering Mongols finally were forced to abandon the invasion.

Kublai had never been one to accept defeat gracefully. Marco Polo and others told him of the wealth of Burma, its gold and silver, its elephants, its stags and roebucks. In 1282, growling with annoyance over the disastrous failure of his second Japanese expedition, the Emperor sent a new army to Burma. The pretext for the invasion was the insult given him by the Burmese king the year before; ten Mongol ambassadors had gone to Burma to demand tribute, but they had behaved discourteously at the royal court, refusing to take off their boots before the throne, and they had been put to death.

The armies clashed, and the Burmese were thrown back. Accustomed now to jungle fighting, the Mongols forced the defenders to retreat steadily down the Irrawaddy River. In 1284 the Burmese capital fell, and the Mongols pursued the fleeing monarch southward for many miles before he surrendered. Burma became part of the Mongol empire, at least to the extent that its rulers sent generous tribute to Kublai's court each year. In fact, Burma remained largely independent; Kublai could not spare the troops necessary to hold it under permanent occupation, and between 1286 and 1301 the Mongols had to invade Burma at least three more times to assert their power there.

Kublai's yearning to conquer the brown-skinned men of the tropics sent Mongol armies into many strange, uncomfortable places in the decade beginning in 1281. The results were usually the same as those in Burma: a Mongol victory after heavy casualties, followed by a reluctant paying of tribute that had to be stimulated by frequent new invasions. Thailand, Malaya, Vietnam, and Bengal on the Indian subcontinent all made grudging submission to the Mongols in this way. So did the distant island of Sumatra. None of these places was ever really under full Mongol control, though Kublai could boast that he received tribute from the lands of the tropics.

Kublai's empire ran from Korea in the east to Tibet in

the west, from the frozen wastes of northern Mongolia to the humid jungles of Sumatra. He had fulfilled the commandment of Genghis Khan, waging unrelenting war on all neighboring lands to bring them under Mongol sway. But Kublai had imposed a great strain on the Mongols, particularly in his catastrophic campaigns against Japan and his costly ventures in the tropics. In his quest for grandeur, the Great Khan had taxed the resources of his people to the breaking point. A day of reckoning was inevitable.

NINE · *The Khan's Last Years*

IN THE Imperial Palace at Peking there hangs a portrait of
Kublai Khan painted in 1291. He had lived seventy-seven
years; for thirty-one of them he had been the Great Khan
of the Mongols, and since 1279 the undisputed Emperor
of China as well. The face of Kublai still shows the strength
of purpose, the vitality, of that other Imperial Palace
painting done in 1265. There have been changes, though.
The rounded face of the Khan now is heavily fringed by
a thick beard. The great drooping mustache entirely hides
his lips. His slanting Oriental eyes are mere slits, and the
man who looks out from them seems solemn and weary,
as though death would not be an unwelcome visitor. It is
the face of a man who has outlived his friends and even
most of his enemies, and who has known such high power,
such total luxury, that life holds no more astonishments for

him. He has sampled every delight and known every sort of grief. His own splendor has come to bore him.

His old age had been marked by bitter reverses. The great rising curve of his life had come in his middle years, from 1260 to 1279, when he had made himself master first of the Mongol world, then of China. Kublai's days had been sweet then. Born in nomad simplicity, with Genghis Khan still alive and in command, Kublai had fulfilled his every dream of opulence. The world was at his feet. Though no longer a young man, he was strong, healthy, able to drink deep from the cup of his success.

As he drew close to seventy, however, the tide began to turn. The failure of his Japanese expedition in 1281 was an omen: even Kublai Khan could know defeat. That same year marked the death of his first wife, Jamui. A year later came the conspiracy against his trusted minister Ahmad and the revelation that the sly Persian had done much to wreck the prosperity of the realm. In 1284 Kublai suffered a more agonizing blow, when his eldest son Chingkim fell ill and died, soon after Kublai had named him heir to the throne. The forty-three-year-old prince had been schooled since childhood to wear the crown of the Great Khan. Kublai had begun to outlive his own sons, and no greater torment could be devised.

He aged swiftly after that. Marco Polo was on hand to see the Great Khan grow old, for Kublai would not let the three Venetians return to their homeland. Whenever they raised the subject of leaving Cathay, the Khan merely told them that he could not spare their services. He seemed to be clinging to them almost desperately, as though he saw in Marco the son he had lost in Chingkim. The Polos performed confidential missions for the Khan and rose high in his administration, and they watched him bend beneath the blows of fortune.

Still, Kublai knew how to take evil tidings philosophically, and he did not give way to self-pity, since he remained the most enviable of men. The hunting expeditions continued, and the great festivals at Cambaluc. Fair-skinned maidens arrived as always to join the harem. Wine and *khumiss* and fine food soothed the Emperor's palate. His collections of curious and delightful objects swelled from year to year, and he did not lose his hunger to learn of other lands and other peoples—a hunger Marco Polo diligently fed.

When in 1284 Kublai discovered that the great island of Ceylon, off the southern tip of India, held certain remarkable sacred relics, he at once sent an embassy to bring the holy treasures to Cambaluc. The relics, according to Marco Polo, consisted of "the sepulcher of our first father Adam, and some of his hair and of his teeth, and the dish from which he used to eat."

Actually there was some disagreement about whose relics were really kept in the mountaintop sanctuary on Ceylon. It was only a Moslem tradition that the hair, teeth, and dish were those of Adam. Christians and Jews believed, as Marco knew, that Adam's burying-place was in the Holy Land, not far from Jerusalem. The people of Ceylon themselves, and most other Asians, thought that the relics were Buddha's. Kublai by this time had come to prefer Buddhism above most other religions, and he coveted these sacred remains of the faith's founder. Marco tells us that "he thought he would get hold of them somehow or other, and despatched a great embassy for the purpose, in the year of Christ, 1284. The ambassadors, with a great company, traveled on by sea and by land until they arrived at the island of Ceylon, and presented themselves before the king.

"And they were so urgent with him that they succeeded in getting two of the grinder teeth, which were passing great and thick; and they also got some of the hair, and the dish from which that personage used to eat, which is of a very beautiful green porphyry. And when the Great Khan's ambassadors had attained the object for which they had come they rejoiced greatly, and returned to their lord. And when they drew near to the great city of Cambaluc, where the Great Khan was staying, they sent him word that they had brought back that for which he had sent them. On learning this the Great Khan was passing glad, and ordered all the priests and others to go forth to meet these relics. . . .

"And why should I make a long story of it? In sooth, the

whole population of Cambaluc went forth to meet these relics, and the priests took them over and carried them to the Great Khan, who received them with great joy and reverence. And they find it written in their Scriptures that the power of the dish is such that if food for one man be put in it, it shall become enough for five men: and the Great Khan declared that he had tried it and found it was really true."

Were the relics genuine? It hardly seems likely. Buddha had lived seventeen hundred years before Kublai Khan, and so many places in the world claimed to have a tooth or a fingerbone of the great teacher that he must have had fifty or sixty fingers and several hundred teeth, if the relics all were genuine. The Christian world, too, was easily convinced of the authenticity of relics, and visitors to Jerusalem in the Middle Ages looked with awe on such things as the "original" crown of thorns, the lance with which the Roman soldier pierced Christ's side, and fragments of the Cross itself.

The relics of Buddha—or Adam—were given a place of honor in the palace at Cambaluc, though no one knows what has become of them today. Whether he believed they were genuine or not, the crafty Kublai knew that the possession of such revered treasures made his city one of the shrines of Buddhism, a symbol of the spiritual and political power that the Great Khan claimed for himself in Asia.

Kublai continued to decorate his palaces with the finest works of Chinese art, too. In this he ran into problems of patriotism, for the greatest painters of the time were southern Chinese loyal to the vanquished Sung Dynasty. The Sung had established an Academy of Painting with a campus in Quinsay. Members of the Academy wore scarlet and purple robes and fish-shaped badges of gold or jade; the Sung Emperors gave them liberal salaries and provided a steady market for the elegant, mistily delicate works of the artists. When the dynasty fell, the Academy of Painting was dissolved and most of the southern Sung artists went into retirement.

As a connoisseur of the fine arts, Kublai Khan tried to persuade these men to pick up their brushes once more. However, they looked upon the Emperor as a northern barbarian, and regarded it as an act of treason against China to paint for him. In 1286 Kublai summoned to his court the painter Chao Meng-fu, a great artist who was related to the Sung royal family. The Great Khan offered Chao a position in his cabinet, as secretary of the Board of War. The duties would be extremely light, and Chao would remain at the capital, painting his wondrous pictures.

For reasons unknown to us, Chao accepted. He left retirement and took up residence at Cambaluc, where he became a great favorite of Kublai. His graceful landscapes and his vigorous paintings of horses and riders soon covered the palace walls. Many of Chao's friends in the south attacked him as a traitor, but when Kublai revived the Academy of Painting in 1287 a few of the retired artists agreed to accept the Great Khan's commissions.

Though the elderly Emperor would have liked nothing more than to pass his remaining days in hunting, feasting, and the appreciation of the arts, his repose was disturbed by a violent and dangerous uprising in 1288. His old enemy Kaidu, who had been in continuous rebellion for more than twenty years, had found a new and powerful ally, and they had vowed to push Kublai from his throne of comfort and restore the true Mongol way of life.

Kaidu's ally was Nayan, the lord of what is now northern Manchuria. His territory extended from the eastern borders of Mongolia to the sea, and from the cold northern forests to the frontier of Kublai's realm. This bold, vigorous young man was a distant cousin of the Great Khan: the great-great-grandson of Genghis' half-brother Belgutai. Nayan was a Nestorian Christian, and his flag bore the Cross.

Marco Polo relates, "When he found himself in authority this Nayan waxed proud in the insolence of his youth and his great power; for indeed he could bring into the field 300,000 horsemen. . . . Seeing what great power he had, he took it into his head that he would be the Great Khan's vassal no longer; nay, he would wrest his empire from him if he could." Nayan sent messages to Kaidu, saying he was "making ready to march against the Great

Khan with all his forces, and he begged Kaidu to do likewise from his side, so that by attacking Kublai on two sides at once with such great forces they would be able to wrest his dominion from him."

Kublai heard of this alliance and was greatly disturbed. Kaidu moved toward him from the west, Nayan from the east. Already they had taken possession of that valley in the north where Genghis Khan and other Mongol heroes, including Kublai's own father and mother, lay buried. Quickly the Great Khan sent couriers to the south, where Bayan, the conqueror of Sung China, was waging war on the Burmese frontier. Bayan was ordered to march north at once to deal with Kaidu. As for Nayan, Kublai announced a startling decision: he would go to battle in person to quell the young upstart's rebellion!

The Great Khan was seventy-four years old. He had not taken part in combat since 1264, when he had defeated Arik-buga. But now he saw the most serious threat to his power since that civil war, and he felt that only by leading his troops himself could he show the Mongol world that he still held authority. "So swiftly and secretly were his preparations made," Marco declares, "that no one knew of them but his Privy Council, and all were completed within ten or twelve days. In that time he had assembled 360,000 good horsemen, and 100,000 infantrymen—but a small force indeed for him, and consisting only of those that were in the vicinity. For the rest of his vast and innumerable forces were too far off to answer so hasty a summons."

In the summer of 1287 Kublai led this army against Nayan. He rode in a well-upholstered chamber carried on the backs of four elephants of war that moved in perfectly coordinated steps. Behind him rode horsemen and spearmen, and the troops dragged along a ponderous fire-*pao*, or bomb-thrower. They marched for twenty days through the northeastern country where Kublai was accustomed to hold his yearly hunting parties. The Great Khan's army arrived so rapidly at the rebel camp that Nayan's men were caught by surprise.

Battle trumpets sounded, and the wild cries of Mongol soldiers taking the field. Above all other sounds came the booming of the *nakkara*, the Mongol war-drum, a brass caldron covered with buffalo-hide, four to eight feet across and carried on the back of an elephant. The din of the *nakkara* was the signal for battle. Kublai led his team of elephants right into the thick of things. Arrows fell like rain, and the blasts of the fire-*pao* added to the distress of the rebels. "From this side and from that," Marco Polo says, "such cries arose from the crowds of the wounded and dying that had God thundered, you would not have heard Him! For fierce and furious was the battle, and no quarter was given."

The rebels fled. Nayan was captured and was brought before Kublai, who ordered him put to death. Since he was of the family of Genghis Khan, Nayan received an execution of a special sort: he was wrapped in a carpet and "tossed to and fro so mercilessly that he died," according to Marco. "And the Khan caused him to be put to death in this way because he would not have the blood of his imperial line spilled upon the ground, or exposed in the eye of heaven and before the sun."

The fall of Nayan did not end the rebellion. Hatan, one of Nayan's followers, continued the uprising in Manchuria, and for three years remained at large until he was hunted down in 1291. In the west, Kaidu drew back when he saw how Kublai had smashed his ally. An army led by the valiant Bayan forced Kaidu to retreat. Though Manchuria and Central Asia remained unruly for the rest of Kublai's life, the threat of his overthrow was ended. When the Great Khan returned from his surprising military exploit in 1288, the courtiers at Cambaluc could not conceal their awe at the completeness of his triumph.

Never again did Kublai Khan go to war. Even hunting lost its pleasure for him. He remained at Shang-tu much of the time, scarcely attending to the business of government. His time was drawing to a close. Beyond the gilded palaces of the Emperor, the realm was plunging into confusion, the paper money almost worthless, the peasants perishing by millions of starvation. The younger Kublai Khan would have taken quick measures to remedy the troubles, but the old, gouty man on the throne had lost contact with his empire, and his courtiers shielded him from the worst news.

The Grand Canal was finished now. The great water-

way linked the Mongol capital of Tai-tu or Cambaluc with
the old Sung capital of Hangchow or Quinsay. Unexpectedly, Kublai decided to make a pilgrimage to Quinsay
to visit the tombs of the Sung Dynasty, his predecessors as
China's rulers. Once more he mounted the luxurious chamber atop the trained elephants, and a lavish procession made
its way southward, following the highway that ran beside
the canal. Deep into China the old man rode, while thousands or perhaps millions of his subjects gathered at points
along the route to stare and to try in vain to catch a glimpse
of the legendary figure within the curtained chamber.
Kublai inspected the resting-places of the overthrown
Emperors and nodded in admiration at the splendor of
Quinsay. Then he returned to Cambaluc, exhausted by his
journey, and withdrew to an inner room of his palace to
recover his strength.

In the first month of 1292 the noonday sky was darkened by an eclipse of the sun: a bad omen. Kublai's Chinese astrologers, fearful of catastrophe, urged him to pray
for heavenly guidance. The veteran general Bayan, seeing
the death of Kublai foretold, worried about the breakup of
the empire once the Great Khan was gone. Bayan urged
Kublai to name his successor. The Emperor selected his
grandson Timur, the son of dead Chingkim.

A few months later, an attack of gout sent Kublai to
bed, his feet and hands throbbing with pain. The King of
Korea, who was paying a ceremonial call on the Great

Khan at Cambaluc, told him that certain sorcerers of his land were skilled at healing such ailments. Kublai had little faith in witchcraft, but he agreed to let the Korean sorcerers try to heal him. They were admitted to the imperial bedchamber, and held Kublai's hands and feet while reciting their chants and prayers. Kublai could not help laughing at the uselessness of the treatment.

He still could laugh, but he saw death drawing near.

The three Polos of Venice also were aware that Kublai's life was ending. Skilled as they were in the ways of the Orient, they knew they might be in danger once Kublai had passed from the scene; favorites in one reign could readily become outcasts or prisoners in the next. Kublai had shown them the kindest of treatment, and in their long years in his service they had acquired great wealth in jewels and gold. Niccolo and Maffeo were old men, and homesick. Marco was nearing the age of forty; he had spent more than half his life away from Venice. It was time to return, now, while they still had the chance. After Kublai's death the homeward road might be blocked forever.

Several times the Polos had asked to be dismissed from the Great Khan's service, and Kublai had refused to entertain the idea. "Nothing on earth would persuade me to let you go," he said, for he found them so useful and likable. In 1292, though, an opportunity arose for them to leave, and they seized it.

The wife of Arghun, the Il-khan of Persia, had died. In her will, she begged Arghun to take no other wife except from her own tribe, the Mongol group known as the Bayauts. Arghun sent ambassadors to his grand-uncle Kublai, asking the Great Khan to select a fair maiden from the Bayauts and send her to Persia to be his bride.

A seventeen-year-old Bayaut princess named Kokachin was chosen for Arghun. About that time, though, Kaidu's uprisings made it risky for the ambassadors to return by the land route with Princess Kokachin. And they feared to travel by sea, since they had no experience with the routes. They asked Kublai to provide them with guides who could accompany them on the sea-voyage to Persia.

Marco Polo returned by sea from a mission to India just as these stranded ambassadors were requesting guides. He hastily suggested that, in view of his long experience in sea travel, he would be pleased to conduct Princess Kokachin to her future husband. His father and uncle would go with them; and, since Persia was closer to Venice than it was to Cambaluc, the homesick Polos would simply continue on to their native city.

Kublai protested. He still did not wish to part with his Venetians. Finally he yielded. Marco, Niccolo, and Maffeo would be permitted to leave. "He called them all three to his presence," Marco Polo's narrative relates, "and gave them two golden tablets of authority, which should secure them liberty of passage through all his dominions, so that wherever they went they might receive provisions for themselves and their attendants. He entrusted them with messages to the King of France, the King of England, the King of Spain, and the other kings of Christendom. He then caused thirteen ships to be equipped, each of which had four masts and could spread twelve sails."

The leavetaking was a sad one. Old Kublai grasped the hand of Marco Polo for the last time, and wished him well. Seventeen years had passed since Marco had first arrived at Shang-tu; it was ten years before that when the elder Polos had first greeted Kublai in the prime of his life. These three Europeans had seen the Great Khan build the world's largest empire, had witnessed the shattering failure of his Japanese expeditions, had been beside him in grief and in joy, had received generous gifts from Kublai and had taken part in his great feasts. Now the time of parting had come.

The ships put to sea from a Chinese port. The huge, slow-moving vessels took three months to reach the island of Java, and made their way westward into the Indian Ocean, where they wandered for eighteen months more. Several of the ships were wrecked, and many lives were lost. Two of the three Persian ambassadors died during the voyage. When the Polos reached Persia in 1294, after many vicissitudes en route, they discovered that Arghun Khan himself was dead. The young Mongol princess became the bride of his son Ghazan. The travelers remained for nine months at the court of Ghazan Khan, and eventually went on to Constantinople, reaching Venice by the end of the year 1295.

They had been absent more than twenty years, and, so the story goes, no one recognized them at first. They had all but forgotten their native language, and in their Mongol clothes they seemed strange and alien figures on the streets of Venice. They proceeded to their house and identified themselves to their relatives. Still there was doubt in Venice that these men were the Polos who had departed so long before—or, if they were the Polos, that their fabulous stories of Mongol grandeur were true.

Ramusio, the sixteenth-century Italian geographer who edited and published a version of Marco Polo's book, tells the story of how the Polos proved the truth of their fantastic adventure. They invited all their kinsmen, says Ramusio, to a sumptuous banquet. "When the hour arrived for sitting down to table they came forth from their chamber, all three clothed in crimson satin, fashioned in long robes reaching to the ground such as people in those days wore indoors. When water for the hands had been served, and the guests were seated, they took off those robes and put on others of crimson damask, while the first suits were by their orders cut up and divided among the servants. Then after partaking of some of the dishes they went out again and came back in robes of crimson velvet, and when they had again taken their seats, the second suits were divided as before. When dinner was over they did the same with the robes of velvet, after they had put on dresses of the ordinary fashion worn by the rest of the company.

"These proceedings caused much wonder and amazement among the guests. But when the cloth had been drawn, and all the servants had been ordered to retire from the dining hall, Messer Marco, as the youngest of the three, rose from the table, and, going into another chamber, brought forth the three shabby dresses of coarse stuff which they had worn when they first arrived. Straightaway they took sharp knives and began to rip up some of the seams, and to take out of them jewels of the greatest value in vast quantities, such as rubies, sapphires, carbuncles, diamonds, and emeralds, which had all been stitched up in those robes in so artful a fashion that nobody could have suspected the fact. For when they took leave of the Great Khan they had changed all the wealth that he had bestowed upon them into this mass of rubies, emeralds, and other jewels, being well aware it was impossible to carry with them so great an amount in gold over a journey of such extreme length and difficulty.

"Now this exhibition of such a huge treasure of jewels and precious stones, all tumbling out upon the table, threw the guests into fresh amazement, insomuch that they seemed quite bewildered and dumfounded. And now they recognized that in spite of all former doubts these were in truth those honored and worthy gentlemen of the House of Polo that they claimed to be; and so all paid them the greatest honor and reverence. And when the story got wind in Venice, at once the whole city flocked to the house to embrace them, and to make much of them, with every conceivable demonstration of affection and respect. . . .

"The young men came daily to visit and converse with the ever polite and gracious Messer Marco, and to ask him questions about Cathay and the Great Khan, all of which he answered with kindly courtesy. And as it happened that in the story of the magnificence of the Great Khan, which he was constantly asked to repeat, he would speak of his revenues as amounting to ten or fifteen *millions* of gold; and in like manner, when recounting other instances of great wealth in those parts, would always make use of the term *millions*, so they gave him the nickname of Messer Marco Millions."

While the homeward-bound Polos had been sojourning at the Persian court of Ghazan Khan in 1294, the news that they feared had overtaken them, carried by swift couriers out of Cathay: the Great Khan Kublai had died.

The last year of Kublai's life had been darkened by one final defeat. Soon after the Polos had called at the island of Java in 1292, Kublai had sent an ambassador there to demand that Java pay homage to him. The ambassador, a

Chinese named Meng Ch'i, was sent back with his face branded like a thief. Kublai responded as he had done two decades earlier when Japan mocked his demands: he commanded that a fleet be assembled to invade and conquer the defiant country. In January 1293 a Mongol navy sailed from the port of Fo-kien. It reached Java late in the year and carried out a landing; but the invaders were driven off with a loss of three thousand men, and had to give up the enterprise. Kublai was gravely disappointed. He had hoped to add one more dominion to the Mongol realm before he died.

In the tenth month of 1293, a comet flashed through the heavens over Cambaluc, frightening the populace and sending the astrologers to Kublai's bedside to warn him that the omen, like the eclipse of the year before, was an evil one. Kublai already knew that. He was dying. He lay cloistered in his palace at Cambaluc, unable to ride forth on his hunting elephants, unable even to wander in the gardens he loved so dearly, where trees from all over Asia had been transplanted to please him.

His Polos were gone. He had outlived his brothers by thirty years. His son Chingkim was in the spirit world. The wife of his youth was only a memory. When he closed his eyes he could see the fierce figure of Genghis Khan standing before him, calling him to account for his long stewardship of the empire. Kublai knew that in many ways he had departed from the *yasas* of the World-Conqueror. Yet he had ruled in splendor, and had been loved by his people, and had tasted victory many times. He did not fear what Genghis might have to say to him in the next world.

They were all gone, the fiery Mongols of Kublai's youth, Ogodai and Chagadai and Tului, Batu of the steppes, cold Kuyuk, hearty Mangu. Arik-buga, Hulagu, Subotai, Bereke—all in their graves. He felt as though he had lived forever. How many cranes had his falcons brought down? How many bowls of *khumiss* had he drained? How many enemies had his warriors slain? The years blurred into a misty haze. He could remember his brother Mangu magnificent on the throne, and his mother Syurkuk Teni glowing with pride—and he could see Mangu dead before his time. He could look back and remember men with white faces coming to him out of the West and becoming as dear to him as his own family. He could see the child who had been Emperor of China knocking his head against the palace floor and hailing Kublai as the Son of Heaven.

All years became this year, yesterdays merged into now. The Great Khan was dying. He called his general to his bedside—Bayan, who had won China for him. Bayan, who had grown old in Kublai's service, found the Great Khan lying on a balcony of his palace, staring at the green pines of his garden. They spoke few words. The Great Khan was a helpless old man, and what could Bayan say?

On the eighteenth of February 1294, in the eightieth year of his life and the thirty-fifth of his reign, the spirit of Kublai Khan parted from his body. By his decree, his corpse was carried in a solemn procession to the north, to the Mountain of Power, and he was laid to rest in an unmarked grave somewhere near the tomb of Genghis Khan.

TEN · *The Aftermath*

THE GREAT KHAN was dead, but no khuriltai was held to
select his successor. The Mongols no longer observed the
old traditions. It was only eighty-eight years since the first
khuriltai, in 1206, had elevated Genghis Khan to power
and set the Mongols on their road to conquest, but in that
time they had come to throw off their ties to custom.
Chiefly it was the doing of Kublai Khan, who had been
born just eight years after that first khuriltai. Kublai had
chosen to think of himself as a Chinese Emperor, not as a
Mongol Khan. While he had conquered China, China had
also conquered him.

So there was no general journey of Mongols to the ancestral homeland, no gathering of gay tents on the bleak
plain, no boisterous festival. The Mongols were scattered
too widely now, and the network of family relationships,

though it still existed, was not the same tight bond it had been when a few brothers ruled the empire. In China, Kublai's grandson Timur mounted the throne by right of inheritance, not by election, and became Great Khan of the Mongols and Emperor of the Chinese. Ghazan Khan in Persia took notice of the event. The Golden Horde sent cordial but cool congratulations from Russia. Kaidu, still rebellious in his mountain strongholds, refused to recognize Timur Khan, but that did not matter.

Timur was pious and moderate. He did his best to check the confusion that had sprouted in the empire during Kublai's declining days. By imperial decree, no one could be put to death until Timur himself reviewed the sentence. Officers who permitted their soldiers to loot the crops of peasants were punished. Timur dismissed from office eighteen thousand bureaucrats who had exploited the people.

The lamas of Tibet, who had won high places in Kublai's regime, pressed Timur for favors. He gave them privileges, but refused to outlaw other religions. The Confucianists, who had been shunted aside in Kublai's reign, were restored to their positions. Christians were welcomed at court. In 1295, Friar John of Montecorvino arrived there as a missionary. He was a Franciscan, like those two great travelers of half a century before, John of Plano Carpini and William of Rubruck. Fifty-year-old John of Montecorvino was the Pope's ambassador to Asia; he came with the purpose of converting Nestorian Christians to the Catholic faith.

Timur allowed John of Montecorvino to build a Roman Catholic church at the capital. He was so successful as a missionary that in 1307 Pope Clement V gave him the handsome title of Archbishop of Cambaluc. The Great Khan himself came to the Christian services now and then. Archbishop John reported in 1307, "I have built a church in the city of Cambaluc, in which the king has his chief residence. This I completed six years ago; and I have built a bell-tower to it, and put three bells in it. I have baptized there, as well as I can estimate, up to this time some 6000 persons. . . . And I am often still engaged in baptizing.

"Also I have gradually bought one hundred fifty boys, the children of pagan parents, and of ages varying from seven to eleven, who have never learned any religion. These boys I have baptized, and I have taught them Greek and Latin after our manner. . . . Eleven of the boys already know our service, and form a choir and take their weekly turn of duty as they do in convents, whether I am there or not. . . . His Majesty the Emperor moreover delights much to hear them chanting."

Timur Khan also dealt with some of the unfinished business of his grandfather's reign, sending armies against Kaidu and the Burmese. Kaidu died in 1301, a rebel to the last. Burma was brought under Mongol control. If he had been given a life as long as Kublai's, Timur might have been a great ruler. Death took him in 1307, though, and his successors lacked strength of purpose.

In the next quarter of a century, six Mongol Emperors came and went. The blood of Genghis Khan was running thin, and this new breed of Mongols, unfamiliar with the hard disciplines of the steppes, was a race of short-lived weaklings. Fevers and drunkenness carried them off. Chaos flourished in China. Famine engulfed whole provinces; rivers burst their bounds and drowned millions; the paper currency became utterly worthless; the Chinese looked with hatred on the Tibetans and Syrians and Uighurs and Arabs who governed them in the name of the collapsing Mongol dynasty.

The handwriting on the wall was clear. The Mongols had built their incredible empire so swiftly because of their obedience to a common plan, because of their physical courage and toughness, because of their inner core of stubbornness and dedication. Kublai Khan, raised in a nomad tent, bore the stamp of those early Mongol ways, and so he had not been overwhelmed by the temptations of China. His descendants, though, lacked the iron of true Mongols. They had never known what it meant to ride day and night for weeks at a time through barren, snow-swept country, or to live on uncertain supplies of milk and meat. Kublai had taken the Mongols out of the steppes and made them city-dwellers, and while he could withstand the change of environment, his successors could not. Kublai the magnificent had sown the seeds of Mongol doom.

The Emperors of the Yuan Dynasty had lost control of China. Rebellions burst out everywhere. Harried Mongol garrisons were sent here, there, crisscrossing the vast realm in a hopeless attempt to suppress every uprising. The government crumbled. The Great Khan of the moment stayed behind the walls of Cambaluc, hoping that the ultimate catastrophe would come some other year.

Through all this chaotic time, Archbishop John of Montecorvino labored on at Cambaluc, writing sadly home that "I myself am grown old and gray, more with toil and trouble than with years." Other priests came to aid him. The most famous was Odoric of Pordenone, who traveled through Asia from 1317 to 1330, and who wrote a book of his wanderings almost as colorful as Marco Polo's. Odoric lived at Cambaluc for three years, and was a witness when the current Great Khan kissed the Cross before Archbishop John. In 1328 the Archbishop died, but other missionaries came.

Merchants came too, for even in the declining days of the Mongol dynasty it was still possible to cross much of Asia without risk. The customary route led from the port of Tana on the Black Sea overland across the heart of Asia, going from the domain of one Mongol prince to the next. About 1340, a traveler named Francesco Balducci Pegolotti of Florence wrote a handbook to guide Italian merchants, and commented, "The road you travel from Tana to Cathay is perfectly safe, whether by day or night, according to what merchants say who have used it."

A time was coming when that would no longer be true. The Chinese had begun to whisper that the Decree of Heaven had been taken from the Yuan Dynasty, and that it was an appropriate moment to overthrow the Mongol masters. Tohan Timur, the tenth Mongol Emperor of China, was on the throne when the uprising came.

Its leader was Chu Yuan-chang, a man of peasant stock so ugly that people nicknamed him "the Pig Emperor." Toughened by poverty, robbed of his family by famine when still a child, he enrolled in one of the many underground rebel groups in China. In 1356, when he was twenty-eight years old, he held the rank of general, and led the triumphant war against the Mongols.

Between 1211 and 1279, in their often interrupted but always victorious conquest of China, the Mongols had moved southward in a series of stages. Now the path of that conquest was reversed, and the stages were much more rapid. The Mongols found themselves being pushed out of city after city, forced northward toward the Great Wall. The widespread Mongol forces, always outnumbered by the Chinese, were powerless now that determined foes confronted them. A mass revolt all over the realm saw peasants falling upon Mongol and other foreign administrators and assassinating them no matter how great the risks.

By 1368, Tai-tu itself, Marco Polo's Cambaluc, was surrounded by the forces of Chu Yuan-chang. Abandoning his capital without a fight, Tohan Timur slipped away and headed for the prairies of Mongolia. As he fled, he composed a lament for the empire he had lost:

Oh, my vast and noble city, my Tai-tu!

Oh, my cool and delicious summer city, my palace of Shang-tu! Green prairie of Shang-tu, where my godlike ancestors lived in happiness!

I allowed myself to drop into dreams—and lo! My empire was gone!

My wondrous city of Tai-tu, built of the nine precious substances by Kublai!

My Shang-tu, union of all perfections, place of endless repose!

Ah, my fame! My glory as Great Khan and Lord of the Earth!

When I used to awake and look forth, how the breezes blew laden with fragrance, and all was beauty and splendor!

And you, my great and noble companions, faithful in all your works! You, my much-loved people! All, all have been snatched from me!

Alas for my illustrious name as the Sovereign of the World!

Alas for my Tai-tu, glorious work of the immortal Kublai! All, all is lost!

The flight to the north continued. The Mongol ministers gathered around Tohan Timur, reminding the poetically inclined monarch, "This is the realm of your great ancestor

Kublai. You must maintain it to the death." Tohan Timur had no taste for battle. Weeping, wringing his hands, he left China behind and made his way to the old Mongol capital of Karakorum, where he died two years later. The soldiers of Chu Yuan-chang drove the remaining Mongols like frightened sheep through the Great Wall.

A new dynasty, the Ming, was proclaimed, with Chu Yuan-chang as its first Emperor. Not for hundreds of years had all of China been ruled by a man of Chinese birth. Centuries of pent-up grievance exploded in a blazing hatred for all things foreign. The Tibetans and Uighurs and Arabs were driven out. The Christian missionaries were expelled. The caravan routes linking East and West were closed. China hid behind a bamboo curtain, unwilling to have anything to do with the outer world. It was almost two hundred years before Europeans returned to China—Spanish and Portuguese explorers who came by sea. So thoroughly had China shunned contact that it was a hundred years more before Europe realized that the realm of yellow-skinned men they reached through the Pacific was one and the same with the Cathay that Marco Polo had entered from the other side.

The Mongols became nomads again. Their time of glory, only a brief moment on the roll of history, was ended. Now and then they ventured through the Great Wall to raid the thriving cities of Ming Dynasty China, but their attacks came to nothing. Eventually Mongolia became merely a

Chinese province. To the Mongols, weak, hungry, and divided, the memory of Genghis and Kublai was a bitter reminder of lost splendor, so remote that it had begun to seem like a dream. All their empires were gone—the Persian Il-khans overthrown by rampaging Turks, the Golden Horde shattered by the fury of the Russian people, down-trodden so long.

For a flickering instant of time the horsemen of the north had threatened to conquer the world. A single family, rich with dynamic personalities, forged an incredible Asiatic empire, bringing order out of confusion, welding a hundred kingdoms into one.

The presence of one great realm that reached from Korea to the Danube left its imprint on history in many ways. For the first time, men and ideas could pass freely from one end of Asia to the other. Arabs, Russians, and Venetians resided at the Chinese capital, while Chinese and Mongol travelers penetrated the Western world. Tabriz, in Persia, the lead-ing commercial center of the Near East, had a large Chinese population in Mongol times. So did Moscow. An envoy from the Persian Il-khan named Rabban Sauma, born in Peking, visited Rome, London, and Paris in 1287, and brought news of Europe back to Asia, just as Marco Polo soon would be doing in the opposite direction.

The flow of cultural change went two ways. The Mon-gols learned about catapults from the Crusaders and about gunpowder from the Chinese; and eventually Europe had gunpowder and cannons, and the Mongols had great slings for hurling bombs. The Franciscan friars who visited the Orient brought back descriptions of the delicate Chinese paintings, and helped to alter the stiff, unrealistic art of Europe; the muraled walls of the Franciscan chapels at Assisi show the influence of Oriental styles. The Persian historian Rashid-ad-Din, whose account of the Mongol empire was well known in medieval Europe, provided a clear description of the Chinese art of printing, and inspired experiments in the West. Marco Polo, too, brought back books from China printed from blocks of wood, and may have helped to set in motion the train of ideas that led to the European development of printing.

Over the routes from East to West and West to East passed many things: drugs, musical instruments, spices, mechanical inventions. The world was knit close by the presence of the Mongol empire, and though the routes were open only little more than a century the exchange of ideas had continuing effects in both worlds.

It is also possible that the existence of that Mongol empire had something to do with shaping the history of the New World. But for Kublai, the great adventure of Marco Polo would never have occurred. The book that Marco wrote was published in many editions during the Middle Ages, and one of its most avid readers was a Genoese seaman named Christopher Columbus. The Columbian Library at

Seville, Spain, treasures to this day Columbus' own copy of Marco Polo, with marginal notes in the great mariner's handwriting. His mind was full of dreams of Cathay when he set out on his long struggle to find backing for a westward voyage. When he sailed at last, and found the island of Hispaniola, he was sure it was the *Cipangu* or Japan of Marco Polo, and that Cuba, which lay beyond, was the coast of Cathay. Columbus hoped to be able to present himself at the court of the Great Khan, whose empire must surely still endure though two centuries had passed since Marco wrote.

And during the greatest years of this empire, its master was Kublai Khan. The lord of Xanadu was a complicated man, Mongol by birth and Chinese by inclination, a wise ruler flawed by grave weaknesses, a shrewd politician and a capable leader, a sophisticated barbarian, far-sighted and short-sighted all at once. To Marco Polo he was a hero beyond compare, "the most mighty man, in respect of subjects or lands or treasure, that exists in the world, or ever has existed from the time of our First Father Adam until this day." To us he is Kublai the magnificent, the glittering, fascinating, paradoxical grandson of Genghis Khan, who presided in splendor over a now-vanished empire that has not lost its power to capture our imaginations.

Bibliography

CREEL, HERRLEE GLESSNER. *The Birth of China*. London: Jonathan
  Cape, 1936.
GERNET, JACQUES. *Daily Life in China on the Eve of the Mongol
  Invasion*. London: George Allen & Unwin, 1962.
GILES, HERBERT A. *A Chinese Biographical Dictionary*. Shanghai:
  Kelly & Walsh, 1898.
GOODRICH, L. CARRINGTON. *A Short History of the Chinese People*,
  3rd edition (Harper Torchbooks). New York and Evans-
  ton: Harper & Row, 1963.
JUVAINI, 'ATA-MALIK. *The History of the World-Conqueror*.
  Translated by John Andrew Boyle. Cambridge: Harvard
  University Press, 1958.
LAMB, HAROLD. *The March of the Barbarians*. New York: Double-
  day, 1940.
LATTIMORE, OWEN. *Inner Asian Frontiers of China*, 2nd edition.
  New York: American Geographical Society, 1951.
NEWTON, A. P. (editor). *Travel and Travellers of the Middle Ages*.
  London: Routledge and Kegan Paul, 1926.

OLSCHKI, LEONARDO. *Marco Polo's Asia*. Berkeley and Los Angeles: University of California Press, 1960.

PLANO CARPINI, JOHN OF. *The Voyage*. Included in *The Principal Navigations Voyages Traffiques & Discoveries of the English Nation*, edited by Richard Hakluyt. Modern edition, Glasgow: MacLehose, 1903.

POLO, MARCO. *The Book of Ser Marco Polo the Venetian*. Translated and edited by Colonel Sir Henry Yule, 3rd edition, revised by Henri Cordier (three volumes, including Addenda). London: John Murray, 1920–29.

———. *The Travels of Marco Polo*. Translated by R. E. Latham. Harmondsworth, England: Penguin Books, 1958.

POWER, EILEEN. *Medieval People*. Harmondsworth, England: Penguin Books, 1937.

PRAWDIN, MICHAEL. *The Mongol Empire, Its Rise and Legacy*. London: George Allen & Unwin, 1961.

REISCHAUER, EDWIN O., and FAIRBANK, JOHN K. *East Asia: The Great Tradition*. Boston: Houghton Mifflin, 1958, 1960.

RUBRUCK, WILLIAM OF. *The Journal*. Included in *Purchas his Pilgrimes*, edited by Samuel Purchas. Modern edition, Glasgow: MacLehose, 1906.

SANSOM, GEORGE. *A History of Japan to 1334*. Stanford: Stanford University Press, 1958.

SILVERBERG, ROBERT. *The Great Wall of China*. Philadelphia: Chilton, 1965.

SYKES, PERCY. *The Quest for Cathay*. London: A. & C. Black, 1936.

WILLETS, WILLIAM. *Chinese Art*. Harmondsworth, England: Penguin Books, 1958.

Index

Index

209